Emily's Legacy

Emily's Legacy

Howe Library's First Century

Patricia Wood Eckels

Emily's Legacy: *Howe Library's First Century*

by Patricia Wood Eckels

Published by The Howe Library Corporation, Hanover, New Hampshire

Printed in the United States of America

Hardcover edition first printed May 2003

ISBN 0-9729066-1-4

Library of Congress Control Number: 2003103602

Design: Desktop Studio

Printing: R. C. Brayshaw & Co.

For purposes of preservation and safe-keeping, papers and photographs in the Howe Library archives were moved to Rauner Special Collections at Dartmouth College in 2001.

Front Cover:

Miss Emily Howe (1853–1912), circa 1885

photograph courtesy of Dartmouth College Library

For all the generations of women and men
whose vision and energy created this very human institution.
And for those who will keep it strong
over the next hundred years.

"The last five letters of the word 'history' tell us that it is an account of the past that is about people and what they did, which is what makes it the most fascinating of subjects."

— Historian Stephen Ambrose
in *To America*, Simon and Schuster, 2002

Contents

Bookplate designed for the Howe Library by Sidney Lawton Smith in 1921. Smith was a renowned designer and engraver. A collection of his bookplates for libraries and private collectors, going back to 1890, is found at the American Antiquarian Society in Worcester, Mass.

Introduction and Acknowledgements

By training I am neither a writer nor a historian, but a librarian. Asked by the centennial committee to attempt this history of Howe Library, I agreed because to me its evolution over the course of a century is an intriguing story and I wanted to share it with others. It has been a labor of love.

In many respects Howe has changed vastly—in size, scope, funding sources, and technology, to name a few. But its metamorphosis from small, quiet, somewhat elite, privately funded book dispensary to bustling center of technological development and community activity may represent only a fraction of the change likely in the next hundred years. Indeed, if we could come back and visit in the year 3000 we might well be more astonished than Emily Howe would be if she dropped in today. But, at heart, Howe has remained, and I hope will continue to remain, what Emily intended it to be: a blessing to this community. And a place to curl up with a good book.

I have consulted all the records available. Sources include one hundred years of Board and Corporation minutes, statistical and financial reports, newspaper clippings and microfilm files; Library studies and surveys that have survived; personal recollections, both my own and those of others; Library newsletters and brochures; and, most helpful for "flavor," the long anecdotal reports written by the Librarians for the Corporation each year from the mid-1930s through 1987.

I have done my best to be accurate. But some records are missing, some are contradictory, and the older ones (official minutes were handwritten until the mid-1960s) are sometimes difficult to decipher. Any quotations not otherwise attributed come from Board or Corporation minutes. I am grateful for the help and advice of many people along the way, but the responsibility for errors and omissions is solely mine.

Three friends whom I grandiosely christened my "editorial board" initially kept me on track in this endeavor. Cynthia Barton is herself a *real* writer and, as a relative newcomer to the community, brought a welcome fresh perspective. Dale Bryant is a former Trustee and long-time Library volunteer whose keen mind drives straight to the point. Peggy Hyde, an active user of Howe since her childhood, is a former staff member who thoroughly understands the Library and its culture. All three read and re-read drafts of this book; they helped me to focus on the important events and provided morale-building encouragement and laughter in times of slow progress. Cynthia was able to stay with the project right to the end, proof-reading and critiquing various "final" versions, which was invaluable. Thank you, Cynthia, Dale and Peggy.

My heartfelt thanks also go to the following people: Former staff member Diane Haas Walker, now doing free-lance editing in the Northwest, used her skills and computer expertise to give the work its initial shape. Marilyn Crichlow, my liaison with the centennial committee and later the Board, provided limitless patience and help over a long gestation period. Former Trustee Phil Friedman volunteered to research the membership of the Board from 1900 to 1965, meticulously intrepreting all those hand-written records.

Wayne Brochl and Nancy Heffernan guided us in learning how a manuscript becomes a printed book and also made valuable editorial suggestions, and Wayne kindly wrote the updating postscript. Director Marlene McGonigle and the present Howe staff were responsive and helpful throughout; Assistant Director Ellen Lynch cheerfully attended to details large and small in ways too numerous to mention. The Rauner Special Collections staff at Dartmouth College assisted in making available the Howe materials now housed there.

My husband, David T. Eckels, who was always certain I could accomplish things I myself had doubts about, encouraged me to begin this project and would have been so pleased and proud to see it completed.

Finally, I want to thank Nancy Des Coteaux of Desktop Studio for the professional skills, the care, and especially the heart she has put into making this book a reality and a thing of beauty. Books and libraries matter deeply to Nancy. No fledgling author could ask for a more sympathetic designer.

– PWE
March 4, 2003

ONE

A Lady's Legacy

1900 – 1916

EMILY HOWE's name is probably better known to today's Hanover residents of all ages than that of any other woman from our town's distant past. Given that we know almost nothing about her as a person, this is a strange twist of history. But Emily Howe's legacy is the Library she provided and endowed and which still bears her name. This is the story of that Library: its years in the Wheelock "mansion" and the move into its present quarters, the people who guided and nurtured it through a century of dynamic change and growth, and its role in the community and among the libraries of the town and the state.

"A blessing to this community"

In March of 1900, according to Hanover town records, "Emily Hitchcock Howe, occupation Lady, age 47," and "Hiram Hitchcock, Hotel Proprietor, age 67," were married in a ceremony performed by Dartmouth president William Jewett Tucker. Both Hiram Hitchcock and Emily Howe were familiar figures in the town. Emily, who had

DARTMOUTH COLLEGE LIBRARY

Emily Howe and her mother leave their house for a horse-and-buggy outing, circa 1890.

lived all her 47 years in Eleazar Wheelock's "mansion house" on Wheelock Street, was the daughter of Benjamin P. Howe, proprietor of a local bookstore and bindery. Hiram was a first cousin of Emily's mother, and had long been a summer resident of Hanover.

Born in Claremont, New Hampshire, Mr. Hitchcock was a prosperous retired businessman and philanthropist. At the time of their wedding he had already given the Mary Hitchcock Memorial Hospital to the community in memory of his first wife. One of his holdings was the Fifth Avenue Hotel in New York City where the couple planned to live after their wedding, returning to Hanover for the summers.

A few weeks prior to her wedding, knowing she would be moving with Hiram to New York, Emily (perhaps inspired by Hiram's beneficence with the hospital and by her father's profession) made the decision to give her family home to the town of Hanover as a library.[1]

1. The history of the Wheelock Mansion from its construction in 1773 until 1900 can be found in Margaret McCallum's chapter, "The Chain of Libraries," in *Hanover, New Hampshire: a bicentennial book*, edited by Francis Lane Childs, 1961.

Hanover's new Library, located at 4 West Wheelock Street, was dedicated on February 22, 1900, and chartered as a corporation by the legislature of New Hampshire. Since her husband-to-be was to chair the Howe Library Corporation, Emily Howe formally presented the deed of the old Wheelock Mansion to him at the dedication ceremony

> *"... with a heart full of the most sacred memories, mindful of the visible associations with the name and fame of the builder...and the prayer that this library may prove a blessing to this community to the remotest generation."*

These prophetic words seem to be Emily's only surviving direct expression of her personal hopes and dreams for her legacy.

On April 6, 1900, after a remodeling planned and supervised by the college architect, Charles A. Rich, the *Hanover Gazette*

BOSTON GLOBE

Howe family residence as it looked after remodeling, 1900

announced that the Howe Library would be "thrown open to the public for the delivery of books" the following day. When the Library opened the next afternoon, young Blanche Poole, daughter of the local dentist, was its first patron. "Being informed that a note from her parents would be necessary," the *Gazette* later reported, "she quickly procured such certification and returned in good season to be the first to draw a book."

The first Trustees of the Howe Library, elected from among the 19 members of the original Corporation, were all male and represented the aristocracy of both Town and Gown. Hiram Hitchcock was chosen as president, and the other Trustees included

> *"the prominent Faculty and business residents of the town: President Wm. J. Tucker of Dartmouth College; Dr. W. T. Smith; Prof. J. K. Lord of the department of Latin; Prof. C. F. Richardson of the department of English; N. A. Frost, jeweler; Prof. T. W. D. Worthen of the department of Mathematics; H. J. Weston of Storrs and Weston, merchants; P. R. Bugbee, cashier of the Dartmouth National Bank; L. B. Downing, druggist; C. P. Chase, College treasurer and president of the Dartmouth National Bank; George Hitchcock."*

Hiram Hitchcock lived only nine months after his marriage. He died in December of that year, leaving Emily a wealthy woman. She then was elected to serve on the Board, but there is no record of her attendance at any meeting until 1903. Charles P. Chase took over the presidency of the Board, a position in which he served for the next 24 years.

"Last Saturday 133 books were drawn"

The Trustees hired Mabel Read, for a salary of twelve-and-a-half cents an hour, to serve as Howe's first Librarian. That she must have performed her duties satisfactorily is indicated by the hourly increase of two-and-a-half cents she was given in July of that first year.

This first Board appears to have met approximately quarterly; they kept rather sketchy records of their actions. The Librarian was not included in these meetings but submitted her written report (usually just an account of petty cash transactions and gift books added) to be read by one of the Trustees.

The Library over which Miss Read presided looked essentially as it had in its years as the Howe family home, complete with heirloom furniture and family portraits. It was open from two to four on Saturday afternoons and provided a collection of about 1,200 books, gathered from various private libraries around town. The *Gazette* noted that

> *"several collections of old books are specially prized for their age and sentiment, especially a few small volumes found in the partitions during repairs, the character and age of which show that they once belonged to President Wheelock by whom they were probably stored away for safe-keeping and then their whereabouts possibly forgotten."*

For its first 12 years the Library's income, produced by renting rooms on the upper floors of the building to bachelor college professors, ranged from $700 to $3,000 annually. These funds appear to have been designated primarily to building repairs and maintenance, as the collection was garnered mostly from private gifts and the Librarians' salaries were nominal.

Storytime in the garden of the Library, sometime between 1900 and 1913. Story-teller unknown.

During those first twelve years there were few changes in the Library's resources or operations, but the Librarians' brief reports do yield some glimpses of its daily activities.

In 1902 the Saturday hours were lengthened into the evening and Miss Read noted, "Last Saturday 133 books were drawn." That year she classified her 111 regular Library users as 10 men, 11 boys, 56 girls and young women, and "34 women presumably beyond the age of 24." In 1903 Charles Chase's wife Fanny joined Emily Howe on the Board of Trustees, and the Library began opening Wednesday afternoons. In 1904 Miss Lois Edith Chandler, now the Librarian, wrote in her report that "only two people have given any difficulty in collecting overdue fees." Minutes reveal that she then proceeded to name the two culprits but mercifully their names were not recorded.

Miss Harriet Storrs was appointed Librarian in 1905; she would continue serving in that role until 1913. By 1906 Miss Storrs could report 727 borrowers; a yearly circulation of 5,185; a total collection of about 1,600 books; and a budget of $750, of which $52 was her salary. At some point during this period, a book committee was established by the Board to handle questions concerning day to day operations of the Library. When Miss Storrs declared that she would like to be informed "how long the $.15 fee entitles college students or high school students who live out of town to draw books" the matter was referred by the Trustees to the book committee.

That same year the first book purchased from the Mabel Read Fund was added to the collection. The Read Fund was the first of

Bookplate for the Library: first named endowment fund.

Howe Library's named endowment funds; it was intended to augment the collection and is still listed today among the Library's assets.

In 1907 the Librarian's salary was increased from $1.00 per week to $1.50, and volunteers began compiling "a catalog of books owned by the Library." Nine books were purchased that year (costing a total of $4.42) but most additions continued to be gifts from private libraries.

A sleepy village Library awakens

The year 1912 brought major changes for the Library. Emily Howe Hitchcock died, naming the Library she had founded as residuary legatee of an estate of approximately $150,000. Both of Howe Library's visionary founders were now gone but, with the advent of increased funding, their legacy would begin to take on a much more substantial role in the life of the town.

This was the beginning of a new era for Howe. Now that there was an income beyond the funds produced by renting the upper rooms to "bachelor gentlemen" there would be monies for actual purchase of books. The by-laws were revised, and the book committee would now be called the library committee. This committee's official charge was to

> *"purchase all books, magazines, newspapers, etc., within the limits of funds available for that purpose; prepare the rules for the management of the library; supervise the cataloging, labeling, and shelving of the various publications; have general charge of the book rooms, suggest suitable persons for employees (except janitor) and fix the duties of the same; require a list of all gifts, purchases, and losses to be kept by the Librarian, and verify his (sic) statements of the same."*

From this it is clear that to date Howe's Librarians had had no formal training and little was expected of them except to preside over the Library during open hours and keep records.

Now, with the increase in funds, a decision was made to appoint a trained Librarian. Miss Etta Clark, who came to Howe from the Middlebury College Library, was offered the position at an annual salary of $1,200, and in 1913 she began what proved to be a seminal policy of service to the community and its children. The Trustees later wrote of Miss Clark,

> *"She grasped at once the possibilities of the colonial Wheelock mansion for the setting of a village library, and much of the charm and restfulness of the interior is due to her thought and taste. She devoted herself very assiduously to building up the collection of books and expanding the work of the library in various directions. Always interested in work for children, it was under her guidance that a definite juvenile department was added. During her ten years as Librarian, the Howe Library developed into one of the outstanding libraries of New Hampshire."*

A month after Miss Clark's arrival in 1913 the Trustees called a special meeting and, at her request, voted to "secure a cataloguer for a period not exceeding four months, at a salary not to exceed $60 a month." They also voted "that the North West room of the Library be set apart and fitted up for use of the children at an expense not to exceed $450." And plans were discussed for building a brick book stack addition onto the Library.

At what must have been one of the most significant meetings of the Board in Howe Library's hundred-year history, decisions were made to have the Library professionally cataloged, to create a children's department, and to provide storage space for the growth of the collection. A short time later the Trustees decided to begin holding their meetings at Mr. Chase's bank rather than at the Wheelock mansion. With the advent of a trained Librarian, they were becoming less involved in the daily life of their Library.

In 1914 the two-story brick book stack was duly added at the rear of the building, with Mr. Bixby as architect and Mr. Hunter as contractor. Library hours were increased from two to four days a week, nearly tripling the circulation between 1913 and 1915. The complete budget was included in the minutes of the annual Howe Library Corporation meeting for the first time in 1915 and showed the grand amount of $1,800 per year budgeted for books and magazines, more than the total annual budget just a few years earlier.

However, the Library's growth brought increased responsibility. It was in 1915 that Alice Ruth Lothrop fell through the opening designated for the book lift in the new Library stack annex. She sued the Library's building contractor for $1,500, and in 1916 the Trustees voted to reimburse Mr. Hunter $1,000 toward his legal costs in settling the Lothrop suit.

Miss Clark wrote to the Trustees in 1916 stating "the desirability of a second assistant in the Library, who shall be a trained librarian and especially fitted for children's work." The position was authorized, with an annual salary of $780. Unfortunately we have no record of who this first children's librarian was or when she began work.

TWO

Signs of the Times

1917 – 1949

Community life and the Library

By now, "the movies" had become part of the Hanover cultural scene, providing the same challenge to the appeal of books and libraries that television would later become. At that year's annual meeting, the Librarian displayed a chart showing small drops in circulation each month since the Moving Picture Theater had opened.

Our country was now involved in "The Great War," and the Library made its own contribution to the war effort. The Trustees voted to allot $112 to the American Library Association as part of a project which "hoped to collect from each town a number of dollars equal to 5% of the number of inhabitants" to provide libraries at World War I army camps.

Newspaper clippings and photographs of the time convey that the Howe Library had become much more than a place to borrow books. Many readers found the coziness, warmth, and charm of the home-like reading rooms a great attraction. In the spring

Front hall and circulation desk, early 1920s. The wildflower table begun by Miss Clark and continued by Miss Kingsland is in right foreground.

Hanoverians used the wildflower table in the front hall to share the flowers they had found in the woods, each vying to be first to spot a species. The Librarian kept "bird lists" on which Library users noted their first spotting of various returning birds each year. Residents loaned their special collections to share with the community (carvings, dolls, autographs, candlesticks, Victorian card cases, and postage stamps, to name a few.) Howe's long tradition as a community gathering place was being established.

In 1921 the Trustees contracted with Sidney L. Smith, noted engraver and bookplate designer, to develop a Howe Library bookplate. Mr. Smith's design, for which the Trustees paid $150, is still in use today. Open any Howe Library book and you will find his graceful depictions of the Connecticut River and the Wheelock Mansion carefully pasted on the first blank page.

Two years later, "yielding to a desire for travel and wider experience," Miss Clark resigned and moved to Washington State. Trustee President Charles Chase contacted Miss Grace Kingsland at the New Hampshire State Library to ask for recommendations of suitable candidates to replace Miss Clark. To his surprise (and presumably to his delight, as she was highly qualified for the position), she offered herself as a candidate. He accepted her offer, and the indomitable Miss Kingsland was hired at a salary of $1,800, to begin February 19, 1923. Thus began her extremely professional and, as it turned out, somewhat autocratic reign of 23 years at Howe.

Sadly, Charles Chase did not live to see the results of his decision; he died the following year, and Ashley K. Hardy was elected to succeed him as the new president of the Board. At this time Miss Mary Fletcher's name begins to appear as a member of the executive committee of the Board, although no woman had yet been elected an officer. Chase's wife, Fanny, elected to the Board in 1903, was serving as chair of the library committee, a position she held until her death in 1934.

In a memorial tribute to Mrs. Chase the Trustees later wrote, "A native of Hanover and lover of books...the esteem in which she was held in the town, was of great importance in maintaining the Library in the cordial regard of the community." Fanny Chase and her husband had both been close friends of Emily Howe and their presence on the Board was generally viewed as providing "a direct link with the founder."

In 1924 we see "Librarian and Staff—$3,800" listed at the head of the budget for the first time. In previous years such items as Furnishings, Garden, and Flowers had topped the list. Miss Kingsland's report that year expressed concern about cramped conditions in the children's room, and the Trustees voted "to contact an architect about the possible enlargement of the building to provide better accommodations for the children's books and staff work room."

The following year a 12' by 14' office was made at the end of the front hall, and what had been the office and workroom, at the southwest corner of the building, became an extension of the children's room. Not only would the small new office/workroom serve as the only work space for Library staff throughout the explosive growth of the next 50 years, but it also provided the only access to restroom and drinking water in the building. This design flaw proved to be a bone of contention throughout Miss Kingsland's tenure and continued to be problematic until the Library moved to its new quarters on East South Street.

Reaching out

In 1927 Miss Kingsland initiated what was to become the long tradition of Howe's service to schools, visiting all the rural schools to share "40 books every boy or girl should read." A summer nature reading club was then begun for grades four through eight. In 1928 the Trustees allocated $100 for the staff to attend State Library meetings, the first mention we have of attention to staff development and interlibrary cooperation. By 1930 the Library was open daily except Sunday, from one to nine, and a book box had been placed on the front steps for deposit of returns at other hours.

Until this time available records tell much more about the maintenance and repair of the building and the financial transactions of the Board than about what was actually happening in library service. Written reports of the library committee no doubt carried this information but have not survived. Typed copies of the Librarian's annual report to the Corporation have been preserved from the early thirties on, however, enabling us to know that the following outreach services were initiated in the 1930s and continued for many years:

Schoolroom collections were chosen and sent out to each grade, and Librarians visited the schools for book talks. Howe Librarians gave instruction in the use of the Library to the upper grades, who were brought to the Library in groups. High school students who commuted into Hanover were allowed to use the Library in the mornings, when it was not normally open. In addition, books were chosen by the Librarian and sent to the hospital, where volunteers took them around to the wards each week.

In 1933, with the New Deal underway, Howe participated in the statewide collection of good reading for young men in the Civilian Conservation Corps forestry camps. "Their main recreation in winter" the Trustees noted, "will be reading and shoveling snow." We are told that Hanover's contribution was one of the largest in the state.

By now children's services were being expanded as well. In 1933 the children's librarian gave ten story hours in the Library for children of school age. She also conducted five additional story hours at rural schools.

The Librarian gains a voice

Grace Kingsland, who served the Library from 1923 until her retirement in 1946, was a true professional. She attended librarians' conferences in other parts of New England and in New York State, and she did her best over the years to prod the Trustees to think beyond the Howe Library as being an historic and somewhat elitist cultural monument. She championed the ideal of library service to everyone and considered the work Howe Library did with students its most important contribution to the community.

Yet she was also a contradictory figure, both admired and feared. Known as a martinet, she brooked no disturbance (even

Grace Kingsland, Librarian 1923–1946

coughing) in her Library and relaxed her rules for no one (including children). Perhaps the most famous instance of this intractability lay in her refusal to allow any member of the public to use the building's only restroom, which was entered through her office. She was notorious for having caused one small boy to create a puddle on the floor while his desperate mother pleaded an emergency.

It is in the records dating from the early thirties that we first begin to see glimpses of Miss Kingsland's formidable personality. In 1934, for example, an inventory recorded that 48 books were missing. We can almost hear the shock in Miss Kingsland's voice as she reports her appalling discovery that the largest number of these were from the gardening section

Circulation, which had been increasing throughout the thirties, reached a high of 65,101 in 1934. Miss Kingsland wisely attributed this increase to the Depression. As libraries across the nation were discovering, increased unemployment meant people had more time to read, and the free public library provided affordable recreation.

In 1935 the Library lost the last surviving member of the original Corporation, Perley R. Bugbee. Mr. Bugbee had served as treasurer of thc Board for 35 years and had also served as secretary

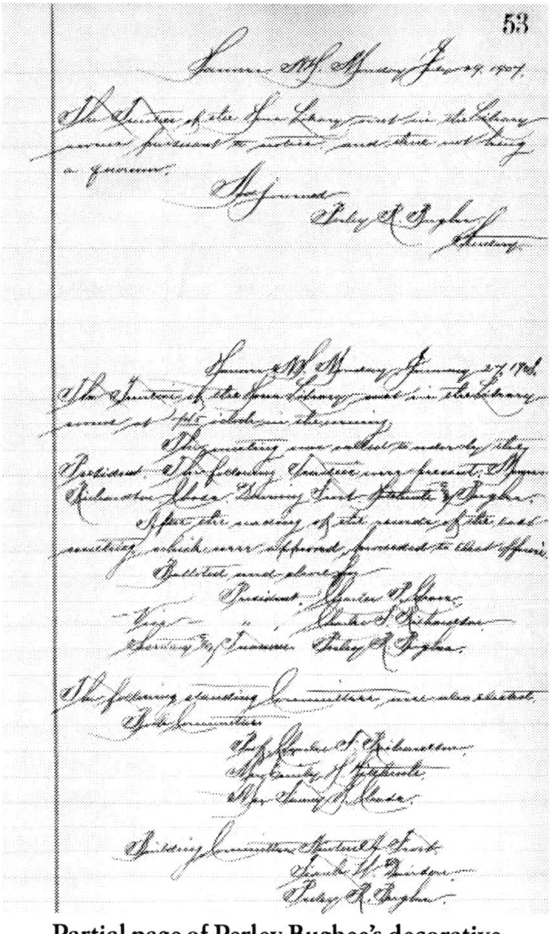

DARTMOUTH COLLEGE LIBRARY

Partial page of Perley Bugbee's decorative but difficult-to-decipher minutes.

until 1916. Unfortunately for research purposes, Mr. Bugbee kept the Board's minutes in a visually beautiful but frustratingly illegible Spencerian script. Some of the mysteries of those early meetings may never be fully revealed. James P. Farnam succeeded Mr. Bugbee as treasurer.

It is perhaps a sign of this "changing of the guard" that finally, in 1936, Miss Kingsland "appeared before the Board" to deliver a report in person. Prior to that time Librarians' reports had been read by a Trustee, as Librarians were not permitted to attend Board meetings. All communications between the Librarian and the Board had occurred either in writing or through working directly with the library committee.

In that 1936 report, Miss Kingsland again expressed her distress that "someone is still taking gardening books without the formality of having them charged." Records note that soon after this report she provided a table displaying gardening books at the Hanover Garden Club's annual flower show, an early instance of Howe's history of cooperation with civic organizations. We can only speculate on whether Miss Kingsland may also have been motivated by a desire to remind the unknown garden-book thieves that they were depriving a whole community of useful information.

Howe Library had been a public library since its inception. Even though it was privately supported and governed, the Corporation had been established expressly for the purpose of maintaining a free library for the use of the people of Hanover. But the question of how to handle non-resident use, still an issue today, arose often. Because there was no tax support involved, the Trustees were free to make whatever policy seemed right for the Library, without regard to equity for Hanover residents.

Through the years they had been quite liberal in their decisions in this matter, and in 1937 they issued their first comprehensive policy statement on the subject:

"Those eligible for free borrowing are residents of Hanover and Norwich, commuters employed in Hanover, residents of West Lebanon Road to the Wilder turn, pupils from out of town attending Hanover schools, transients in Hanover or Norwich. All other persons shall make a special deposit equal to the value of the books borrowed... For the guidance of the Librarian it is here stated that it is the opinion of the trustees that residents of neighboring towns who want books for study purposes need not make a deposit unless there is some question about their reliability."

Perhaps reliability had proven to be an issue with Dartmouth's student population, as the policy statement specifically noted "Dartmouth students will be served only through loans to Baker Library." Clearly the Board—or Miss Kingsland—preferred to have Baker responsible for Howe's loans to the college students.

In 1938 the Library was closed for six weeks in the summer for redecoration and repairs. While putting in a new ceiling in the adult reading room that summer, workmen discovered an unexpected reminder of the building's origin as Eleazar Wheelock's home—the date "1773" was found, carved on one of the large structural beams.

"Should we make more effort?"

Miss Kingsland, by 1939, was openly expressing her concerns, not only about the Board's separation from the running of the Library, but also about the Library's separation from the larger community. During her report that year, in a wry but telling comment, Miss Kingsland suggested the Trustees consider holding the annual meeting of the Corporation in the children's room at Howe instead of at the bank. "It has always seemed unfortunate to me that these meetings had to be held outside the Library building which they concerned, when it is the one time in the year that some of the members might see the inside of the building."

In that same report she also addressed the somewhat elitist stance of the Library. In a plea for what today's librarians call "outreach," she asked,

> *"Are we too passive in our attitude towards people coming to the library? It has always been the policy to provide good books, a competent and interested staff, pleasant surrounds, but to do little outside publicity. Should we make more effort to reach the non-reading group? Have we any responsibility for the continuing education of adults who need some encouragement?"*

Despite Miss Kingsland's concerns for education, it seems clear that the understanding in the community was that serious informational needs would be served by the "big library" across the Green, as the doors and the book stacks of Baker Library were at that time open to the general public. In contrast Howe Library, during this period, existed primarily as a source of leisure reading for the Hanover community; adult fiction represented approximately 74% of the annual circulation. Accordingly, in 1940, a rental collection was begun to finance the expansion of the mystery collection on the theory that such volumes were "necessary for the relaxation of the academic minds" in the community.

Miss Kingsland's efforts to encourage cooperation between the Library and the community often proved to benefit the Library and its collection as well as the community at large. There is frequent mention in her reports from this era of the Garden Club members who were bringing in flowers from their own gardens and arranging them in the Library, a sharing that continues to this day. The early tradition of treating the Library's reading rooms as a space to share treasures with neighbors persists.

Another form of early partnership between the Library and community organizations, also continued into the present, were the gifts of specialized books and magazine subscriptions donated regularly by a variety of civic groups interested in sharing their enthusiasms and special interests with others.

President Ashley K. Hardy died in 1941 and was succeeded by John B. Stearns. (It appears that in Howe's first four decades death was the only escape from the presidency of the Trustees.) That year, for the first time since 1913, the annual meetings of the Corporation and the Trustees were once again held in the Library rather than at the bank. For the next five years they gathered in the children's room, while the adult section stayed open for business; but beginning in 1946 the meetings were held in the adult reading room, with the entire Library closed to the public. Miss Kingsland had made her point.

By 1942 World War II had brought many servicemen to Hanover to be trained at Dartmouth. In keeping with Miss Kingsland's principles, the Library was quick to accommodate their needs. That year 163 temporary borrower's cards were issued to navy trainees, their wives and children; and a reading area was established in the garden so that navy wives could spend time there with their babies in perambulators. The Library also collected 1,203 books for the USO Victory Book Drive to supply books to the armed forces. But Miss Kingsland did not see service to our armed forces as the only response to the war effort; as always she kept the needs of the community in mind. Her report that year noted that "for the rest of our contribution to the war effort we have tried to bring attention to books which would make clear the democratic way of life and that would help to prepare people for post-war problems."

Hard times

In 1943 circulation was at a low level. During the Depression it had peaked at just over 65,000, but with better times it had begun to decrease and, just before the war, had dipped to about 60,000. Then the war brought more people into the work force, both paid and unpaid, and the resulting loss of leisure caused a further, sharper drop in circulation. By 1943 circulation had fallen to the level of 1927, about 46,000.

Miss Kingsland's annual report also described extensive personnel turnover, resulting in a shortage of staff for much of the year. Howe lost its children's librarian, and staff shortages forced the Library to close two evenings and one afternoon each week.

Soon yet another wartime problem began to surface. The Librarian's report for 1944 cites the increasing difficulty of getting new books in a timely fashion. Also, because of paper and labor shortages, bindings were flimsy, quality of paper was poor, and press runs were smaller and soon out of stock.

In 1945 Howe was without a children's librarian for a second year. Miss Kingsland stayed focused on the community's needs in spite of staff shortages, however. When the war ended she established a special shelf for returning veterans. This included "some of the best books and pamphlets about [postwar] agencies, relations between the veteran, his family and his community, and the rehabilitation of the disabled."

Later in 1945 the Trustees declared a policy of retirement by age 70 for professional staff. Miss Kingsland's long tenure therefore ended in 1946. In "sincere gratitude for her strong loyalty to the Library, her faith in its potential influences, and her abiding devotion to a high sense of duty," the Trustees granted her $1,150, half of one year's salary, which was invested in an annuity for her.

Mrs. Elsie Lilley, who had been an assistant, was appointed Librarian in August of 1946. She immediately suggested that salaries be studied and a salary scale be adopted because of the difficulties of attracting capable people at the salaries then being paid—a theme we were to hear often during the next few years. Mrs. Lilley's written reports to the Trustees during the subsequent months convey a great sense of optimism and enthusiasm, combined with a decidedly practical approach to the challenges she faced in keeping the Library staffed and functioning.

In August of 1946 Miss Mary Steele (years later, as Mary Ermenc, she would be a president of the Board) came to Howe as children's librarian. Her story hours became extremely popular; an attendance of 93 was reported at one. In that same year, with a memorial gift from the parents of Dorothy Jane Guyer, a circulating collection of phonograph records was begun. This was Howe's first venture into non-print media. Another "first" occurred when a "Keen Teen" corner was set up in the adult reading room, the forerunner of the later young adult collection.

By this time the Trustees had become greatly concerned over the inadequacy of the Library's income to meet the current year's budget or to fund the next year's operation. They voted to ask the Selectmen to consider a Town contribution of $2,200 to the Library in the coming year, but their request was denied.

From the mid-forties on there is recurrent emphasis in the Board minutes on the financial stresses caused by both inflation and the ever-increasing demand for service. Repeatedly they struggled with the difficulties of balancing the Library budget given the escalating problems of the postwar years: the challenge of attracting and keeping qualified staff at the salaries offered; the need for a retirement plan, which they could not afford; the constant drain on the Corporation's finances for repairing and refurbishing a very old building, including five rental apartments on the upper floors; and the need to seek financial support from private donors or from the taxpayers. This struggle stood in marked contrast to the first 45 years, when Howe's endowment income seemed more than adequate for its needs.

By the end of 1947 all the staff had left, with the exception of the Librarian herself and the janitor, Mr. Harris. The children's librarian had resigned to attend graduate school; one assistant had departed because her husband had graduated from Tuck School; and the other assistant had done so because she was unable to live on a salary of $99 per month when her rent was $75. Mrs. Lilley wrote, "Now there are only Mr. Harris and me, and if a job were to be offered in California or Hawaii there would probably be only Mr. Harris." The Trustees voted to appeal again to the Town, this time for $4,000 toward the coming year's budget. They also decided to sell several items of value that had been given to the Library earlier, including a collection of the autographs of U.S. presidents.

Mrs. Lilley reported on a "coming out party" in May of that year, a celebration to introduce the eighth and ninth graders to the adult part of the Library; prior to this time they had been restricted to the children's room until ninth grade. She also reported that special shelves at Howe were now stocked with books and magazines relating to topics the various junior and senior high school teachers were emphasizing, as there were still no libraries in any of the local schools. The Library experimented with Sunday hours for the public but, since "the same people came on Sundays as on the other days" this was soon stopped.

Unable to replace the children's librarian because of the low salary, Mrs. Lilley did manage to hire two part-time assistants, but she reported that with this staff she could not keep the Library open 52 hours a week. Hours were reduced to 32 and salaries were increased slightly. That year the Board decided, in spite of "being loathe to change the masculine tradition of the upper floors of the library," to make available an apartment for an assistant librarian if it would help attract qualified staff. They also made plans for creating a Friends group to raise funds in Hanover and Norwich, and they once more voted to approach the Selectmen, who had so far not responded to their pleas.

"I didn't bite the teacher"

In 1949, still without a children's librarian, Mrs. Lilley delivered a highly emotional report to the Corporation. Sounding out of patience and put-upon, she said that the shorter hours were upsetting the public, the staff had no time for their behind-the-scenes work, and she was working outrageous hours. And, she added,

> *"preparing and reading an annual report to Corporation members is just about the most discouraging part of this librarian's work. The effect I get trying to arouse a group of people who are only mildly interested, in most cases, in what I am doing and what the library is doing, is more or less like the reaction of my three-year-old niece to her first Sunday School class. When asked by her grandmother if she liked it, she replied 'Well, yes, I didn't bite the teacher.'"*

Not surprisingly, Mrs. Lilley resigned in March and Miss Frances Haslett, an assistant, was asked to take over. Miss Haslett had come back to her hometown of Lebanon after retiring with the rank of technical sergeant from the Marine Corps. Having become interested in library work while in its Special Services, she was pursuing a master's degree in library science by taking leaves from Howe during the summers.

That same year, Charlotte Ford reported to the Corporation on the activities of the new Friends of the Howe Library group. They had been working to solicit private contributions to the Library and to make people aware of its financial needs. Personally contacting 455 selected cardholders, they had raised about $2,200, the largest single gift being $60. However, the contributors had made it clear they were not willing to commit to annual gifts; they felt the needed funds should come through the Town. One suggested that Howe might merge with Baker Library, an idea hastily rejected by both the Trustees and Dartmouth College Librarian Nathaniel Goodrich. Others suggested that the schools should share some of the financial burden now being born by Howe since "the school budget for library purposes is kept to a minimum (dictionaries, en-

PHOTO BY DAVID PIERCE STUDIOS

COURTESY OF DARTMOUTH COLLEGE LIBRARY

Storytime in the children's room, 1950, Helen Garrison reading.

cyclopedias, etc.) with the knowledge that Howe will assume the usual school library functions."

That year, 1949, the $4,000 from tax funds was finally granted by the Town so that financial pressures were somewhat relieved. This was the beginning of the successful blending of public and private support which enabled Howe Library to grow into the modern public library it is today. But for many more years it would continue to be an independent institution, financed by its endowment, requesting supplementary funds from the taxpayers when the budget could not be met.

In July the former six-day schedule of open hours was resumed. Helen Garrison was hired as children's librarian, finally filling that key position. And Mary Churchill of Lebanon, just graduated from Radcliffe, joined the staff as a full-time clerical assistant doing typing, book processing, and record keeping, beginning her 45-year career as invaluable aide to Howe's Librarians. The Trustees declared at last that "the financial picture is not so bleak as it appeared a year ago."

THREE

Fiftieth Anniversary and Beyond

1950 – 1966

"An old-fashioned book-peddling institution"

IN 1950, because Hanover taxpayers were now paying approximately three dollars per family per year for the Library, the Board voted to charge non-resident borrowers an annual family fee, which they set at two dollars. Failing to find a staff retirement plan they could afford, they voted to waive their exemption under Social Security law and become part of the federal program so that Library personnel would at least have that protection.

In her first annual report we get some insight into Miss Haslett's views on Howe's mission:

> *"I see Howe Library as an old fashioned book-peddling institution, in contrast to the current fashion of public libraries involved in films, discussion groups, and the like. Howe, dominated as it is by Dartmouth and its activities, has no room or place for acting as a clearing-house for social and intellectual fashions. It should cater to children and young people ... Our reference work is generally of a trivial nature."*

Westerns and romances were popular, she reported, but there was little interest in the genre of science fiction. Vinyl LP records were being added to the record collection and the old shellac records were being phased out. Miss Haslett further stated,

> *"I should like to be able to preserve the major contributions of my two predecessors. Miss Kingsland I think was an unusually fine Librarian and may be credited with an outstanding accomplishment in the field of technical librarianship. Mrs. Lilley had a flair for public relations and made a fine library into a popular institution."*

Miss Haslett's only serious complaint about her first year at Howe was

> *"children in the toddling and screaming stage. Parents are conditioned to the uproar that children produce but certainly we in the library are not. Occasionally it is necessary for us to issue an ultimatum—quiet or else. Most public libraries do not allow children inside until they have reached 6 years."*

The Marine Corps does not seem to have prepared Sgt. Haslett for the vicissitudes of public librarianship, but she appears not to have been alone. Thus far in Howe's history there is no evidence of Librarians working with preschoolers, who today serve as a primary clientele for most public libraries, including Howe.

In April 1950 the 50th anniversary of the Library was celebrated. By now there were 52 Corporation members, nearly half of them women, and 12 Board members, of whom two were women. The Friends of Howe Library group had finally managed to raise $2,500 for Howe in celebration of the anniversary. Margaret McCallum chaired a committee which planned a series of special events for the occasion.

Old photos and newspaper clippings concerning Howe were exhibited in the Library for the anniversary, along with some of the earliest accessions. Approximately 100 Friends braved some "very unpleasant weather" to attend an anniversary open house (with punch and cookies) and view the exhibit. Attendees were treated to a talk by Trustee Leon B. Richardson, who spoke "most entertainingly about the early days of the library and gave amusing and sympathetic vignettes of some of the personalities connected with the library in the first years of the century."

A separate anniversary dinner was held at the Dartmouth Outing Club House for members of the Board and Corporation, their spouses, and a few invited guests, primarily present and former staff members. Speakers included Dartmouth President John Sloan Dickey; Nathaniel Goodrich, Librarian of Baker Library; and,

PHOTO BY ADRIAN BOUCHARD

COURTESY OF DARTMOUTH COLLEGE LIBRARY

Howe Library in winter, 1950, with DKE house on the right

Cover of the program for the 50th anniversary celebration

again, Professor Richardson. A pamphlet with an historical sketch written by Professor Richardson was distributed. The total expenditure for the weeklong celebration, which included the printing of 1,200 pamphlets, the invitations to both events and tickets to the dinner; postage; flowers and punch; photographer; and 14 dinner guests at $1.85 each, was just $129.97, well under the $200 budgeted for the occasion. The week's events were generally held to have been a rousing success.

At the annual meeting in January 1951 Miss Haslett reported that the previous year's circulation was the highest ever, which she attributed to the publicity surrounding the anniversary. She then urged the Trustees to contact their representatives in Congress in support of the Library Services Act, which would provide Federal aid to libraries.

In February Miss Haslett was granted a six-month leave of absence to finish her graduate studies before her GI Bill benefits ran out, having assured the Board of her return to Howe for "at least several more years." But that October, her studies completed, she resigned to take a position in Massachusetts. The lure of a higher salary had wooed yet another librarian away from Howe.

Miss Hurlbutt takes over

Mrs. Garrison took over as Acting Librarian but soon announced that she, too, would be leaving to accept a post with a better salary. Dorothy Hurlbutt, a Hanover native who had worked at Howe some years before, had recently returned to Howe as a half-time assistant. In 1952 the Trustees appointed her Librarian at an annual salary of $2,200, a position she was to hold for the next 13 years. Mary Steele Ermenc, now married and back in Hanover, began working part-time. And Helen Stickney, a former teacher, was hired as children's librarian.

At about this time Trustee Edith MacDonald reported on her attendance at an educational session for New Hampshire Library Trustees. Two points had been stressed at that gathering: that there should be more frequent meetings of the Board (they then met quarterly), and that the Librarian should be included in those meetings. After discussion it was agreed that "the Librarian would often be invited to be present to assist in the discussions, but each such attendance should follow a specific invitation. [They] ...wished no binding commitment in the form of a vote, which might at times cause unnecessary embarrassment." This was a telling illustration of the ongoing barrier to a real working partnership between Librarian and Trustees of that era. The frustration expressed earlier by both Miss Kingsland and Mrs. Lilley had not yet been resolved.

Between 1953 and 1955 the Board several times asked Dartmouth Trustees to help with painting and other needed repairs, in view of the building's origin as home of the college's first president; but the college felt that it could not oblige. Finances again became a serious problem.

The Howe Trustees, although having authorized their officers to procure a pension plan for full-time staff, reported to the Corporation that "the pension plan discussed in July cannot now be acted upon." Circulation dropped in 1955 to 65,632, down more than 3,000 from the previous year, and Miss Hurlbutt speculated that this might be due to the growing popularity of television.

After ten years of negotiations Congress at last, in 1956, passed the Library Services Act which Miss Haslett had earlier urged the Trustees to support. The funding this legislation provided produced a boom in library services throughout the United States during the next two decades, and eventually in New Hampshire a statewide system of supportive services for public libraries was established to assist struggling local libraries.

In 1957 a library was finally established at Hanover High School. But Howe continued to work closely with the school, providing for many of its curricular needs while that new library was building its collection. For the elementary grades Howe remained the only library resource until 1965. In a 1959 report to the Corporation, children's librarian Helen Stickney delivered an extensive report on activities in the children's room, but there was still no mention of special work with preschoolers.

National Library Week was first declared in April of 1958. In celebration of the occasion, the Librarian and a Trustee appeared together on the long-time radio program, "Breakfast at the Hanover Inn." For years Howe had been using the *Hanover Gazette* (which generously printed everything Howe gave them, including a weekly column) and, to a lesser extent, the *Valley News* to publicize its services, but this interview was apparently the Library's first venture into radio publicity.

Garden Club members completed their third year of work on the Library grounds in 1959. Still-existing plans of this project indicate that it was a major undertaking.

That year the Trustees appointed a committee, with Margaret McCallum as chair, to work on plans for renovations and repairs to the building itself in preparation for the town's bicentennial in 1961. This committee's ambitious report noted the need for painting the exterior; painting and papering the reading rooms; repairing and refinishing furniture; purchasing some new furnishings (lamps, drapes and rugs); re-gilding the gold frames for the childhood portraits of Emily Howe, her brother, Charles, and sister, Sarah; and establishing a permanent maintenance committee so that maintenance would be budgeted and kept up on a regular basis. Their recommendations were accepted and most of the work was carried out in 1960, with the Library closed for 27 days during the work. Funding was provided by the Corporation.

In 1960 the children's librarian died suddenly. Miss Hurlbutt expressed the shock and loss felt by both staff and public and noted that "while not a professionally trained librarian, Mrs. Stickney knew children and their books and was full of interest and enthusiasm in her field." Elizabeth Hayward of Lyme was appointed to the position in September. She had an undergraduate degree in librarianship from Simmons and had worked at Baker in earlier years, but had had no experience working with children. The Board noted that "trained children's librarians are scarce, and too expensive for Howe's budget."

Overflowing with books and young people

Board of Trustees minutes in 1960 recorded the concern of Trustee S. John Stebbins who "objected to the extreme brevity of recent Trustee meetings. He felt some pressing matters required careful study." At the annual meeting of 1962 Mr. Stebbins' concerns were addressed when a committee was appointed to "study the demands that the library can expect in the next ten years—the books, staff, and plant needed to meet such demands." Jack Stebbins was, of course, appointed to this committee. Over the following years, he worked to awaken both the Board and the Corporation to the need for a long-range plan for Howe, much as he provided similarly farsighted leadership for several other Hanover institutions and organizations.

Dorothy Hurlbutt's report that year makes the first recorded mention of the staff's problem with after-school supervision of students waiting for rides home to Norwich and Lyme. This would be a theme expressed with increasing urgency for years to come. Miss Hurlbutt described the reading rooms as "overflowing with young people and their belongings," with a serious shortage of study space. "There have been one or two parents who have completely forgotten to pick up their children," she remarked in her usual mild way.

The New Hampshire State Library, with federal money available through the Library Services Act, had conducted a survey of library service in the state and recommended a plan for improving it through coordinating the efforts of libraries of all types. As part of this plan a bookmobile from the State Library now began coming to each town several times a year. Librarians could board the bookmobile and choose supplementary collections for their readers of all ages. Even though Hanover's readers were already better supplied with books than many of the state's citizens, the bookmobile provided a welcome boost to the always-strained book budget.

At the annual meeting in 1963 the study committee appointed a year earlier submitted its report. Chaired by Ellen Adams, a former librarian at the college, the committee included Trustee Jack Stebbins, Corporation member Dorothy Gliddon, and Dartmouth Librarian Richard Morin. After carefully considering the Library's role in the community, the state of its facilities and resources, and the demands that could be anticipated within the next decade, their report concluded that "the next ten years should first see relief for crowded book storage and relief for seating shortage for children and high school students."

Among other needs they cited were additional staff, a study of staff salaries, closer cooperation with the high school and its library, a study of acquisition policies in light of the presence in town of the college library, an active campaign for gifts, and a close relationship with the State Library.

Miss Hurlbutt reported that Joan Stewart, a part-time assistant for four years, would like to do graduate work in library science at Simmons in the summer, and the Board voted to pay her tuition.

At the 1963 annual meeting the Corporation enacted the first major revision of its by-laws since 1912, deciding that henceforth the Corporation and the Board of Trustees would have a single set of officers. Professor of English Herb West, in his role as Corporation president, presided over these deliberations. Although his official role was eliminated as a result of the decision, his interest in Howe remained strong. For many years he continued to write astute critical notes that were placed in the new mystery books. (Today, in a few of the older mysteries, you may find two comments: MBMcC and Herb West in friendly disagreement over the evaluation.)

Margaret Beck McCallum
Trustee 1944–1970

The finance committee reported (again) that Howe salaries were low, and that new graduates of library schools were now receiving $5,661 on average. At that time Miss Hurlbutt was still earning an annual salary of considerably less.

During this same year, 1963, John and Jean Meck established the Meck-Hazlett Fund for children's books, in honor of his mother and aunt. Although many one-time gifts had been made to Howe over the years, many of them memorial gifts, this was only the second named book endowment fund ever given, the other having been the Mabel Read Fund in 1906, in honor of Howe's first Librarian.

Margaret Beck McCallum, the Trustee who had chaired the anniversary committee and the bicentennial committee, was named the year's Most Valuable Library Friend by the New Hampshire Library Trustees Association in 1964.

"Twenty years a trustee . . . she has served the Howe Library in Hanover constantly, graciously, and well. Her good taste, good humor, and good sense have directed the course of the library through the many committees on which she has served. For years she has read many of the new books and written short notes to be posted in them, so that many readers have come to depend on the opinions of 'MBMcC'."

Five successive Librarians could enthusiastically attest to the truth of that citation.

"A happy place to work"

In February of 1965 Dorothy Hurlbutt retired. She had come to Howe right after graduation from Mt. Holyoke, served as an assistant from 1922 to 1937, then left for several years to care for aging parents. Returning in 1951 and named Librarian in 1952, she had served 13 years in that role. The Trustees paid

"well deserved tribute to Dorothy Alden Hurlbutt, under whose leadership our library has given mental refreshment, relaxation and stimulus to a constantly increasing number of readers... Under her administration Howe has been a happy place to work, as staff or volunteer."

They voted to pay Dorothy Hurlbutt a pension of $100 per month and to continue their seemingly endless quest for a pension plan they could afford.

A shy woman, never assertive or abrasive, Miss Hurlbutt had perhaps not pushed the Trustees to face some of the problems of growth that were upon them, or to recognize the need for Howe to expand its range of services as public libraries elsewhere were doing. She was fairly satisfied with the status quo and apparently never protested when, after delivering her annual report to the Corporation, she was excused from the room for the Board meeting that followed.

But Dorothy Hurlbutt was a woman who knew and loved books, and she built Howe's collection with a fine discrimination. Those who knew her fondly remember her gentle wit and warm acceptance of her fellow humans.

Joan Stewart was next appointed Librarian. She directed the Library's operation while continuing to take summer leaves to complete work for her master's degree. In her first year Mrs. Stewart made several changes. New lighting was installed in all the reading rooms and the front hall with funding from the Chamber of Commerce and several individuals. Under the leadership of Trustee Tay Burnett, volunteers created a small staff room in the basement. The Friends group, which seemed to repeatedly disband and then appear in a new incarnation, was started again with Joan Stewart's encouragement. She also began issuing an annotated list of new adult books each month.

Mrs. Stewart made two important recommendations to the Trustees. She suggested that gift monies for books, book rental fees, and replacement fees for lost or damaged books should be available to purchase additional books, not used to reduce the book budget as the treasurer had been doing. She also urged the Board to begin planning for an addition to the crowded Library.

That year Howe joined the newly established Statewide Library Development System and was thereby eligible to purchase books through a cooperative plan at a better discount, to receive annual grants to purchase reference books, and to participate in quarterly meetings with other librarians in this part of the state for the purpose of upgrading service to all. The following year,

1966, Howe would be appointed a Service Center Library in this statewide system.

Joan Stewart continued to make changes in 1966. All borrowers were re-registered for the first really accurate count in some years. Of the 2,601 registered, 46% were adults, 23% high school students, and 31% children. Hours were increased so that Howe was open weekdays ten to nine and Saturdays ten to five. Nancy Moorman joined Lari Widmayer, who had come in 1965, as library assistant, each working about three-fourths time. Christopher Kyllonen became the Library's first teen-age page; until his advent circulation staff had been shelving all returned books themselves.

Although a library had been established in Hanover's elementary school the year before, Howe's circulation of children's books still continued to increase, to the dismay of those who had believed that Howe's role as a resource for children would be lessened.

Later that year Mrs. Stewart received her graduate library degree and announced that she would be leaving October 1 to accept a position with a better salary in the Midwest. Replacing her with anyone they considered "acceptable" at the salary offered proved to be so very difficult that from October 1 through the end of 1966 Howe was without a Head Librarian.

In the interim the Board appointed as "Acting Head" Mary Churchill, who had been employed at Howe by this time for 17 years. Miss Churchill, children's librarian Hayward, and assistants Widmayer and Moorman somehow carried the full workload of the day-to-day operation during this period. To ensure that the selection of adult books would continue uninterrupted, the Board appointed a book selection committee made up of three Trustees and former Librarian Hurlbutt. And they continued their search for a Head Librarian.

FOUR

The Transitional Years

1967 – 1970

The beginning of a twenty-year adventure

In autumn of 1966, as the Board continued its search, school librarian Frances Richmond[2] spotted a new volunteer at the elementary school library whom she urged to apply for the Howe position. Patti Eckels had recently moved from Los Angeles to Hanover when her husband accepted a position in the Dartmouth development office. Using Baker Library's resources, she was working independently on the one remaining bibliography course she needed for her graduate degree in library science. But, with four school-age children, she had no immediate interest in a full-time position.

Nevertheless, at Fran's instigation, Trustee Margaret McCallum (known for her ability to charm and persuade) invited Mrs. Eckels to tea and somehow managed to convince both herself and Patti that a neophyte librarian with no administrative experience and a Wellesley BA in psychology could direct a busy library operation while work-

2. Fran had been at Howe Library as a part-time assistant from 1952 to 1954. The Richmond Middle School was later named for this dynamic, creative and much-loved librarian, whose life was cut tragically short.

ing part time. The December 1966 Board minutes report that Patricia Wood Eckels was appointed Acting Librarian, to begin January 1; the following June, when she was to receive her MLS, the word "Acting" would be removed from her title.

It was agreed that Patti would work two days a week, concentrating her efforts on giving overall direction to the Library, selecting materials for the adult collection, and developing the relationship with the new statewide library system. Because she would not be working full time, Howe could afford to pay a prorated salary based on the $6,000 going rate for entry-level professional librarians.

This was the beginning of a 20-year adventure for both Library and Librarian. The Trustees may have often wondered how they had committed Howe to the care of an outlander from California with a head full of new-fangled notions about what a public library could and should be. And the new Librarian, of course, had no real idea of the "mid-life crisis" Howe had been experiencing as it struggled to grow into the role of a modern public library despite its inadequate financial base.

At the 1967 Corporation meeting in late January, Christina Dickey (wife of Dartmouth's president) was elected the first female president of the Board in the Library's 66-year history. At that same meeting treasurer Maurice Aldrich announced some wonderful news. Adelaide Hardy, whose husband had served as president of the Board from 1925 to his death in 1940, had left a bequest of $77,487 to the Library. Then, outgoing president Professor Harry Schultz introduced the new Acting Librarian to the Corporation.

After reporting on the activities of the previous year, Patti thanked the staff for their patience and good humor and applauded the warm affection for Howe that she was finding throughout the community and the quality of the book collections assembled by her predecessors. By this time the collection had grown to nearly

30,000 volumes, and there were 91 current magazine subscriptions, many of them gifts. The annual circulation had reached 78,555.

During those first months Mary Churchill was invaluable in orienting the new Librarian to Howe's systems, helping her sort out who was who among the patrons, and conveying the frugality with which Howe Library operated. When Mrs. Eckels asked about the neat row of paper cups in the restroom, it was Mary who explained that each cup was identified by a staff member's initials scratched on the bottom, and could be used over and over.

A number of changes were made during that first year. The mystery collection, previously inter-shelved with the rest of the fiction, was thoroughly weeded and moved to its own separate section, and a collection of large type books was begun. The new Librarian began conducting storytimes for three and four year-olds. Despite the dangers of the twisting stairwell to the basement staff room where the story hours were held (obviously OSHA did not exist), the response of preschoolers and their parents was enthusiastic. Soon two sessions were scheduled each week.

To help the newcomer-Librarian become more familiar with the needs and habits of the community, a survey was distributed to Library users. Three popular suggestions—a paperback browsing section, an expanded record collection, and a rack for bicycles were implemented within the year. But for the 25% of the respondents who wished for expanded quarters the response would be longer in coming.

During 1967 the Board made two momentous decisions. When Patti Eckels again raised Joan Stewart's question of how gift book funds were handled, she was told by the treasurer that income from the Mabel Read endowment was not an extra fund but part of the general income. This seemed a matter that should be carefully discussed by the full Board. After consideration of the implications of this policy, the Board did vote in July that "all money given for specific purposes shall be considered over and above any amount budgeted for those purposes." This was a landmark decision, resulting in many more gifts to the book fund over the years.

The other decision seemed equally momentous to many. It was decided that the Library's only restroom, previously limited to staff use, could become a public facility open to all ages and both sexes. Miss Kingsland would have been horrified.

A cautious minuet

Hanover's first Town Manager, Neil Berlin, arrived on the scene that year and asked to attend the Trustees' meetings. The Town government was now regularly allotting several thousand dollars to help the Library balance its budget every year; no doubt the Manager felt he should have more input. But the Board decided that "the Library is not public in the usual sense of the word and therefore it would be best to simply invite him to attend the budget meeting of the [Library's] Finance Committee."

At this point David J. Bradley, the Selectmen's liaison to the Howe Board, suggested asking for legal clarification of Howe's status. When a lawyer serving on the Board urged his fellow Trustees not to ask for a definition in writing of their legal status as a public library because it might encourage "public interference in our affairs," they asked the Librarian to discuss this with State Librarian Emil Allen. Mr. Allen assured them that any library in the state that freely serves the public is considered a "public library." However, Mr. Berlin did not push his request to attend Board meetings.

Nevertheless, this exchange marked the beginning of a cautious minuet performed by the Trustees and the Town government for the next several years. The Trustees found it increasingly difficult to meet the changing needs of the times for library service within the limits of their endowment income. Already they were (no matter how reluctantly) having to ask for some tax support each year.

Since 1900, operating with total independence in their decision-making, the Corporation and Board had done a magnificent job of providing high-quality library service to the community. They were proud of this history; they knew their record for library service provided had been far above average in northern New England; and they were somewhat suspicious of what would happen if the "bureaucracy" got its foot in the door. It was understandably difficult for them to relinquish any independence to the Town.

The "bureaucrats," on the other hand, were fiscally responsible to their constituents, the taxpayers. They understandably felt there should be more accountability, more openness on the part of the Board, if the Town were to hand over tax monies at Howe's request each year. As the requests grew ever larger, in spite of the Board's efforts at frugality, the tempo of the minuet picked up. That the dance ended in a way so beneficial that public and private sectors were able to join forces and strengths was due in large part to the basic good will of all concerned. That Hanover's first Town Manager was a man who loved libraries, used Howe frequently, and had the patience and good humor to encourage the Trustees was great good fortune for the community.

"At the invitation of the Trustees"

Howe's involvement in the statewide library system increased in 1968. Interlibrary loan use grew dramatically: 72 books were loaned to other libraries and 125 items were borrowed by Howe for local patrons, tripling the 1967 number of loans. Several staff members attended courses or workshops sponsored by the State

Library. Since most employees of public libraries in New Hampshire had not had any professional library training, these courses filled a real need. Howe's Librarian was appointed to two statewide committees working to improve total library service in New Hampshire. A federal grant, channeled to Howe by the State Library, provided 100 new large type books.

That May, with the Librarian present by invitation, the Howe Board approved its first full set of written policies for the operation of the Library. These had been drawn up by Trustees Margaret McCallum and Dorothy Sampson, working with the Librarian, and covered such areas as personnel, book selection, and the role of the Board.

Included in the policy statement was a provision for the Librarian to be in attendance at all regular Board meetings. When the executive committee unanimously approved the policies before taking them to the full Board, secretary Harry Schultz—ever considerate and courtly—told Patti quietly that she should not take it personally if the provision for the Librarian to be included in meetings were removed, as he thought it might be.

Professor Schultz knew his Board well. It had long been apparent that when important issues arose most of the Trustees looked to the wisdom of long-time treasurer Maurice Aldrich for the decisive opinion. In many ways, no matter who held the office of president, it was he who was the de facto leader of the Board. And, as predicted, he saw this particular policy as a restriction on the Board's privacy and independence. When the Board met to discuss the policies, "at the invitation of the Trustees" was added to the statement that the Librarian would regularly attend Board meetings.

After that meeting the Librarian expressed to Margaret McCallum her concern that the Board's protective attitude towards its "territory" weakened the ability of the Trustees and Librarian to provide unified leadership and that it might some day prevent the Board from attracting a first-rate professional to Howe. Two months later, while the Librarian was on vacation, the Board met again. There is no record of their discussion, but on her return there was a brief note from MBMcC waiting on her desk: "The Trustees have decided to remove the phrase 'at the invitation of the Board' from the policies." Mrs. McCallum had once again asserted her powers of gentle persuasion and quiet diplomacy.

This is perhaps a good place to discuss Maurice Aldrich, his considerable influence, and his very great contribution to the well being of Howe over his years as Trustee and treasurer. He had been elected to the Board and then immediately chosen treasurer in January 1946, and he remained treasurer until his death in 1977. For those 32 years he served the Library with incredible devotion and scrupulous attention to its fiscal well being, husbanding Howe's resources as carefully as if they were his own. Other members of the Board trusted his judgment about the Library's finances without question and most never felt the need themselves to understand the finances at all. He was a man of few words, with an enigmatic smile and a calm, unruffled manner. Each decision was made soberly, thoughtfully, and slowly.

Over the years, those who knew Mr. Aldrich came to appreciate and admire all these strengths. But initially it was hard for the new Librarian not to see him as something of a benevolent despot, standing firmly in the way of progress, though always with the best intentions. For example, it was very difficult for him to accept the idea that Howe needed, indeed must have, a written policy for such matters as sick leave and vacation periods. His feeling was that the Library had always taken good care of its permanent staff and would continue to do so, but he preferred to have nothing committed to paper. In the late 1960s this was not a theory acceptable to staff any more—even to librarians, who had not, in his past experience, been very assertive.

This cautious, slow approach could be very frustrating at a time when major change seemed not only necessary but long overdue. Each time the Board seemed poised to take a giant step forward, Mr. Aldrich's reaction was to have the issue studied some more. And then some more. Because of his long tenure and the history of deferring to his judgment, his approach usually prevailed. However, the time would come when Maurice Aldrich was finally convinced that action must be taken, that the Library must put service first, giving up the beloved old building and moving to a new site. From then on he worked just as tirelessly with Board and Town officials to accomplish this goal as he had always worked to preserve Emily Howe's legacy. Perhaps he saw by then that her legacy was more than a building; it was a tradition of service to the community.

Desperate need

Minutes of the May 1969 Board meeting record that "the matter of exploring possibilities for future expansion of the Library plant... was briefly discussed and not considered immediately urgent." Further discussion was delegated to the executive committee. The year before, in the Librarian's annual report, after reviewing the overcrowding in both book stacks and study areas, she had stated that "the one big question the Library will have to face in the near future is expansion."

It seemed impossible to delay a serious discussion of this problem much longer, so at the next meeting Patti took the Trustees on a tour of the building to illustrate the desperate need for space. While some of the Trustees were regular Library users, there were others who rarely experienced the building first-hand, since their meet-

PHOTO BY DAVID PIERCE STUDIOS COURTESY OF DARTMOUTH COLLEGE LIBRARY

Board of Trustees, 1969. Left to right, seated: Maurice Aldrich, Mary (Tay) Burnett, Elaine G. Harp, Henry Schultz, S. John Stebbins. Standing: Edward C. Lathem, Dorothy H. Leavitt, Margaret B. McCallum, Margaret Sperry, John B. Stearns, Barbara Morin, Patricia Eckels, Joan P. Fowler, William Crooker. Absent: Catherine L. McKennan.

ings were once again being held in the spacious boardroom of the Dartmouth Savings Bank.

After the tour the Trustees voted to establish a study committee at once, requesting that it report to the Board as quickly as possible on space needs. Barbara Morin was asked to form and chair the committee. It was also agreed that the executive committee would begin to meet with the Librarian each month between the quarterly Board meetings, to improve cooperative planning and communication. The relationship between Librarian and Board had begun to move forward.

Other events of 1969 included a celebration of Mary Churchill's 20-year service to Howe, an increase of the annual non-resident fee from two dollars to four dollars, and the acquisition of a film projector to provide Saturday films for children. These films were available on loan through the film cooperative at the State Library. The Library also began giving direct service to Dartmouth students. Like their professors, they used Howe mostly for recreational reading and their numbers were few. But those who wanted to browse and borrow at Howe were grateful not to have to go though formal interlibrary loan channels. To everyone's advantage, the new policy reduced clerical work at both libraries.

Through the late sixties and early seventies, in spite of cramped quarters, the Library always kept a small space in the reading room reserved for topical book displays and book lists. Some highlighted seasonal topics and other light subject matter; others dealt with the more serious issues of the time. These were years of great social and political ferment, and there were displays on civil rights, environmental conservation, the conflict in Vietnam, Afro-American history, population control, the back-to-the-earth movement, and alternative power sources, to name a few.

In 1969 various issues became problematic in the upper apartments. The worst of these were leaky roofs and plumbing problems, which caused water to seep down through three floors into the children's room of the Library. It was described as "a nightmarish tour of duty" for maintenance chair Posey Fowler and her committee. After sorting through water-damaged books, the staff found that insurance reimbursement would replace very few of the items that had to be discarded. Most of the books were old and their value had depreciated far below replacement costs. It was Patti's challenging introduction to the problems of a library functioning as landlord in an antiquated building. But it was far from the last such problem. Elderly third floor tenant Professor Irving Bender, had a distressing tendency to start drawing a tub of water and then go off to do errands in town, leaving the tub to overflow.

"Howe Library—looking ahead"

At the annual meeting of the Corporation in January of 1970, Barbara Morin presented "Howe Library—Looking Ahead," the very thorough report of her committee, whose other members were Trustees Mary Ermenc, Patricia Radway, and Margaret Sperry, and community representative Pegge Strickler, with the Librarian serving as advisor. The report pointed out that use of Howe by young people had increased considerably over the past ten years, in spite of the expansion of the high school library and the establishment of the grade school library. More adults were also using the Library, with total circulation having increased by 40% since the Adams committee study of 1962.

The report carefully considered space needs for both circulating and reference materials; for staff work areas, seating, exhibit and program space; and for such basic necessities as public restrooms.

It also weighed the pros and cons of trying to expand on the present site or building anew on a site that offered adequate space for both a larger library and parking.

> *"To sum up," the committee wrote, "the Trustees should address themselves to the following questions: Whether any enlargement on the present site will meet space needs for the next 20 years; whether problems created by the age of the original structure in terms of safety, maintenance costs and inefficiency of operation would not offset the advantages of remaining on the present site; whether overcrowding of the old wooden building would not affect its historic charm; whether overall costs of an addition plus the cost of renovating the older building would not be commensurate with the cost of a new building; and whether the Town would agree to such an addition because of zoning restrictions and parking inadequacies.*
>
> *"The committee feels we must weigh all these factors against the historical significance of the building and decide which is more important—the building itself, or a library that can render the services that will be demanded of it in the future."*

In conclusion the committee unanimously recommended that "the Trustees hire a professional library consultant to help them determine what course they should take to realize the best potential of the Howe Library to serve future residents of this community." Receiving the report with gratitude, the Board agreed to consider the matter further.

Meanwhile, the Librarian cleaned out the miscellaneous items stored in the closed-off upper level of the stacks, selling some items of value, giving others to the Historical Society or the college museum, and discarding over 2,000 outdated or worn out books among the 3,000 dusty volumes being stored there. In preparation for opening this area to the public, a professional cleaner scrubbed down 50 years of accumulated grime. One bright spring weekend, eight high school students formed a human chain and moved all the non-fiction to the upper stacks. They then redistributed the books remaining on the main level, providing some empty space on each shelf and thus relieving (for both patrons and staff) an intolerable shelving situation.

A new record-browsing bin was built for the Library, replacing the old orange-crate style shelves in which the records had been

Cover of brochure describing Howe's services and policies, circa 1970. Sketch by Walter Roach.

tightly jammed, and a part-time assistant was hired to begin cataloging the collection of nearly 700 recordings. To everyone's dismay, on the day the new record bin was introduced one of the regular older patrons haughtily examined it and declared with disapproval, "Well, it's not very colonial-looking." Had the old orange crates been colonial-looking? Gratifyingly, other patrons found it quite wonderful to be able to see more than the tiny lettering on the thin ends of the record jackets.

By now Patti Eckels' position as Librarian had become full-time. It had, of course, been a delusion to think that the work could be done in two days per week. She had gradually been adding extra days since 1967, and still spent many evenings at home reading book reviews or working on other Library business.

F I V E

Planning for Expansion

1970 – 1974

"The Library must have new quarters"

In June the Board followed the recommendation of the Morin report, contracting with library consultant Emerson Greenaway for a $750 study of Howe's problems. Mr. Greenaway, former head of the Philadelphia and Baltimore library systems and a past president of the American Library Association, was an internationally known library expert. It was Howe's good fortune that he was now retired, living in nearby New London, and feeling a need to stay involved in the library world. His selection as consultant proved to be wise, for he understood not only libraries but also the workings of small New England towns and the importance of including everyone in the process of building consensus. He also knew how to express his ideas clearly without professional jargon and, as staff and Board soon discovered, working with him was a delight.

Mr. Greenaway delivered his report, "The Howe Library and Its Future," to the Board in October of 1970. He assessed and made recommendations about the collections, the staff, the services offered, and the physical facilities. While he praised the staff's competence and its enthusiasm in providing "as many services as the building will allow," he stated emphatically that because of space limitations "there are many services not being given which are accepted as normal programs in other libraries." His first priority recommendation was that, although the venerable building was both historic and charming, "in my opinion the Howe Library must have new quarters to permit full services to the people whom it serves" and to house an adequate collection of materials.

Mr. Greenaway's report stated emphatically that he did not believe there could be enough space on the West Wheelock Street site for adequate expansion, or that the old building could be safely and adequately modified in any case.

That December three Trustees, the Librarian, the Town Manager and a committee of the Selectmen met to discuss ways of acting on certain recommendations of the Greenaway report. And in January of 1971 it was agreed that the Greenaway report would be released to the newspapers and that the Board would discuss with Mr.Greenaway his fee for writing a building program in preparation for expanding or relocating Howe Library.

The Trustees decided to accept the Town's offer to investigate designating the Library staff as Town employees so that they would be eligible for the Town retirement plan. But word soon came back that it was not legally feasible to do this as long as the Library remained a separate entity.

In June of 1971, the Board met with Mr. Greenaway and hired him to work on a statement of building needs at a fee of $125 a day. In November they voted to appoint a building committee to follow up on the building program he and the Librarian had prepared over the summer and early fall. By now the Board agreed unanimously, after hearing from architects, engineers, and other experts, that it was not possible to meet the library needs of the community by expanding on the present site, even if they were to utilize either the DKE house or its site. (They had purchased the DKE property, adjacent to Howe's site, when the fraternity disbanded the previous April, hoping it would be useful in the Library's expansion.)

The following year, 1971, brought a confusing array of staff changes. Children's librarian Elizabeth Hayward, having reached retirement age, was honored at a luncheon in appreciation for her 11 years of service. Pegge Strickler, who replaced her, was an experienced teacher, familiar with children's literature. She agreed to work four days a week and take a series of public library training courses offered by the State Library. Lari Widmayer, resigning to devote more time to her many community interests, was replaced at the circulation desk by Diane Haas, just graduated from Mount Holyoke. Nancy Moorman took an extended leave because of ill-

DARTMOUTH COLLEGE LIBRARY

Children's librarian Pegge Strickler reading to preschoolers in the basement staff room, circa 1972.

ness. Elenita Chickering and Phyllis Phillips temporarily replaced her and continued to work part-time when Mrs. Moorman later returned at reduced hours. Running an operation as busy as Howe and training four people new to library work in the space of a few months was a stretch for all concerned.

Circulation that year jumped 3,000, exceeding 100,000 for the first time. It was now necessary to hold three storytimes for preschoolers each week to provide for all who wanted to attend. Questionnaires were mailed to all Corporation members and 16 volunteers were recruited to help with book mending, inventory, home delivery, and other projects which the already strained staff could not manage. This was the first time volunteers had been used in such a large-scale and systematic way.

"Outreach" was an important theme of the year, with publicity to acquaint non-users with such services as talking books and home delivery to shut-ins and to the local nursing home. For National Library Week Patti Eckels developed a series of 30-second public awareness promotions for which staff member Diane Haas' husband Fred (then a Dartmouth student and now a well-recognized teacher and performer of jazz) composed and played the musical background. These were recorded by WDCR and aired by three area radio stations. And, a happy occasion for all who had long valued her contributions to Howe, Margaret McCallum was again honored by the NH Library Trustees Association, this time as Trustee of the Year.

Responding to new financial challenges

On the financial front, the treasurer reported that the Library would need to ask the Town for an unprecedented $25,000 to make up the projected budget shortfall during the coming year. And, yet again, the Board appointed a committee to look for an affordable retirement plan for Library staff.

The year 1972 was difficult financially. The state had never been able to fund the statewide library system at more than 20% of the intended level. This year, however, there was zero funding, eliminating the $700 Howe had received the previous year for increased book purchases. Also, the Town had not been able to meet the Library's requested budget contribution, forcing the Library to close for two half-days each week and to cut its book budget even further.

In response to the financial challenges, the Board raised the non-resident fee to $5 for New Hampshire residents and $8 for others. And, as proof that an ill wind does sometimes blow good, the Library began supplementing its circulation staff with work-study students from Dartmouth, a practice that has continued ever since. It has saved money, brought some talented young people onto the scene, and inspired a few students to take up careers in librarianship.

On the brighter side, Howe's grant application for federal funding of $4,800 was approved, allowing it (in cooperation with school libraries and community organizations) to develop a collection of audiovisual materials and the equipment necessary to use them. Both materials and equipment would circulate to the public. Howe began to build a collection of spoken word cassette tapes (oral histories, poetry readings, lectures), slides (art history, travel), and filmstrips, the precursors of today's videotapes. Don Hawthorne, audiovisual specialist at the high school, was the Library's knowledgeable advisor on the technical aspects of this project. He also served on the Library Board as the Selectmen's representative.

At Howe's initiative, regular meetings of librarians from the Dresden, Hanover, and Lyme school districts, Dartmouth, Howe, and Etna libraries now began. The group issued a cooperative statement defining the role of each library in serving the community and building complementary, not competing, collections. To this end Howe and the schools began routinely exchanging lists of newly acquired reference books and audiovisual materials and established a union catalog of audiovisuals.

In September the Trustees called a special meeting of the Corporation to further inform members about the Library's need for expansion and to discuss the DKE house. The Board had become convinced that the DKE property could not be used by Howe. They were in a difficult position since, in spite of its terrible condition, the house was the oldest building in town and had great sentimental value to many. However, after hearing the Board's concerns the Corporation members agreed there was little choice but to sell (for removal) or demolish the old fraternity house as soon as possible. Neither Dartmouth College, the Hanover Historical Society, nor any other group felt able to take on its renovation and maintenance, and the empty building had become a safety hazard. The lot was to be kept "for possible expansion," since Corporation members' feelings about the old Library building still made it hard to accept the thought of starting anew on a fresh site.

Something of a bombshell

November 1972 was a turning point. The League of Women Voters sponsored a public meeting to air the question of the Library's future. Anxious to provide basic information to the public before the meeting, the Library prepared a fact sheet for wide distribution, listing the range of Howe's available services, giving comparative statistics for the decades from 1920 to 1970, and highlighting such facts as these:

> *All administrative work, cataloging and book processing must be done in a room 12' by 14' shared by the Librarian, a clerical assistant and a huge information file cabinet. One book must now be discarded to make room for each new book added. The only restroom in the Library is a tiny cubicle reached by going through the Librarian's office. A staff of five must find space to work in a building staffed 50 years before by one Librarian and an occasional assistant.*

Sixty residents turned out for a long and substantive discussion, at the end of which Dr. Harry Bird (chair of the Town's finance committee) suggested that "perhaps the Town should be asked to take over the entire operating budget of the Library beginning in 1973, to indicate whether it would be willing to provide the annual support if the Library used its endowment to build a new, greatly expanded library."

This was something of a bombshell. Selectman Hawthorne then spoke up to agree that this would indeed be a fair indication of the Town's commitment and that he personally would support such a request.

When he repeated this support at the December meeting, the Trustees decided to raise the matter with the Corporation in January. Thus, after great soul-searching and considerable hesitation, the Howe Board ended this busy year energized to move into several even busier ones. The staff was elated at the prospect of real action being taken, since they felt the space crunch more painfully each day.

A doubly gratifying vote

At its January 1973 meeting the Corporation formally voted to ask that an article be put on warrant for Town Meeting asking for total support of the Library's 1973 operating budget. In March the voters unanimously approved the warrant article, appropriating $56,000 for Howe's current budget. For the Board and the staff this was a doubly gratifying vote. Not only did it provide a stable base on which they could build wisely and confidently for the future; it was also a vote of confidence in Howe Library and in the way it was serving the Town. To them, the vote meant the people of Hanover saw a public library as an important part of the services any enlightened community ought to support through its taxes. The Library immediately resumed its 62-hours-per-week schedule, and in July all Howe employees became Town employees, abolishing forever the endless Trustee discussions of a retirement plan.

At a long April meeting the Board discussed Howe's future in terms of the Library's new status within the Town government. What would be the relationship between Board and Selectmen? Trustee Joan (Posey) Fowler urged the Board to appoint a committee to move forward with planning, working very closely with the Selectmen. Also in April, the DKE house was demolished and its site transformed into a parking lot for Howe patrons. Before this there had only been on-street parking.

That June a search committee, chaired by Mrs. Fowler, began seeking possible sites in the event the decision were made to move from the old building. By September they could report that the site at the corner of East South Street and Currier Place was the best one available. Everyone concerned was reaching the conclusion that even if the existing building could be extensively remodeled it would not only lose its charm but also be less than satisfactory from a functional point of view.

Among the influential voices being raised to encourage giving up the community's sentimental attachment to the historic "Wheelock mansion" was Margaret McCallum's. Given her own devotion to the building and its history, this could not have been an easy personal decision. But being a forward-looking woman of great practicality and courage, she was able to put aside her own sentiment for the past when she saw that a move was in the best interest of the Library's ability to function and grow. The persuasive case she made for facing this reality in a special newspaper article undoubtedly influenced many who respected her judgment.

With her sudden death that summer Howe lost a friend of many talents and steadfast dedication. She had once joked, when asked to represent Howe at some public gathering, "I have to be careful, you know—I've been doing this so long that people will begin to confuse me with Emily Howe." It was easy to tell her with perfect honesty that no one would ever confuse Margaret McCallum with anyone.

Many people asked staff members during that transition period, "How do you like being a municipal employee?" The fact was that with Neil Berlin as Town Manager they experienced no interference at all in the way they had been operating the Library. When Patti Eckels approached Mr. Berlin about whether she might accept the State Library's request to teach a ten-session course in Library Administration to librarians in the North Country, making up those hours at other times, he promptly replied, "Of course, go ahead. The state would be a lot better off if more of the libraries were run as well as Howe is." To be sure, some "red tape" had been added to their work; but in exchange they had been relieved of some of the old clerical headaches, such as administering the payroll. And the Librarian found it educational to work with the heads of the other departments and become more aware of the high quality of public service Hanover received from all departments.

The Board was now meeting monthly, a commitment they had long resisted. Minutes of the February 1974 meeting reported that

Selectmen Edgar Mead and Don Hawthorne "expressed the sentiments of the Selectmen that we should not delay a decision any longer. We must find a site and think about fundraising." There followed a long discussion culminating in Jack Stebbins' statement that "not one of the many professionals concerned with the future development of the Library has ever indicated that we can hope to provide first class library service to the town in the present location. We are not fulfilling our trust to the citizens of Hanover by pursuing a program of postponement and procrastination." He then made two motions which passed unanimously: that the Trustees inform the Selectmen that they definitely wanted the E. South Street site for a new Library, and that a committee be appointed to interview architects and report back to the Board.

SIX

Creating the New Library

1974 – 1975

Real action

The snail's pace movement toward real action had certainly been accelerated. In the spring the Board hired the Boston firm of Shepley Bulfinch Richardson and Abbott whose architects began to meet with the building committee.

Posey Fowler, who had been chosen to serve as chair of that committee, recruited the following other members: fellow Trustees Maurice Aldrich, Barbara Morin, and Ruth Young; Town Manager Neil Berlin; Selectman Donald Hawthorne; Director of Facilities for Dartmouth College Gordon DeWitt; Corporation member Philip Krueger; and Librarian Patricia Eckels. Emerson Greenaway agreed to serve as consultant to the committee as needed. The local firm of Trumbull Nelson was chosen as contractor.

In June the architects requested an open meeting for the community to hear about plans for the new Library and express their views. Tentative blueprints and sketches were shown, as well as a scale model of the building. "It's a big building, but in small sections," explained architect James Clapp, who then answered questions from the floor. The building committee stressed the commitment of all involved in the planning that being efficient and state-of the-art must not preclude being comfortable and inviting. "We needn't, and we mustn't, sacrifice the special qualities that have made Howe Library what it is." The response of those attending was encouragingly enthusiastic.

A surprise contribution of $25,000 from James Wicker, a California resident who had grown up in Hanover, gave fundraising a major boost. Shortly after that came a second generous gift, when Dartmouth College pledged another $25,000 to the building fund.

SHEPLEY BULFINCH RICHARDSON & ABBOTT

Cover of the fund-raising mailer used in building campaign, 1974–1975

Earlier in the year financial considerations had caused the college to conclude that it could no longer make circulation privileges available free of charge to everyone in the region who applied for a card. A $100 annual fee had been instituted for anyone not currently connected with the college. Dartmouth's major gift to the community via the Library fund helped to cushion the shock to the "locals" who had so long relied on the generosity of Dartmouth's unusual

Ground-breaking celebration, November 4, 1974, with Harry Tanzi at the microphone. Behind him left to right: Lou Bressett, Edward Brown, Posey Fowler, James Clapp (architect) and John Kemeny. Hanover High School Band is at far left.

open library policy and who would now need to go through Howe to request the college's books on interlibrary loan.

At a special meeting in September, Town Meeting approved, by a vote of 220 to 9, a $490,000 bond issue for the Library, since it could borrow at a lower rate of interest than could the Corporation. The money would be repaid to the town through the sale of the old building and the proceeds of the fund drive. Meanwhile the Town and the Board had worked out an agreement whereby the Corporation would deed the DKE lot to the Town in exchange for a $1.00 per year lease on the new site, which had been purchased by the Town. The lease would be in effect as long as the Corporation continued to use that site for a library.

Later that month the Dartmouth Savings Bank honored Maurice Aldrich on his retirement as Chairman of its Board of Directors. At his testimonial dinner the bank announced its major gift to the Library's building fund and the naming of the reading room in the new Library in honor of Mr. Aldrich. His portrait hangs over the mantel in that room.

In November a groundbreaking celebration was held on the Currier Place site, complete with high school band, hot cider, and many balloons. Mrs. Fowler presided over the ceremony; the speakers were Hanover's Honorary Mayor Harry Tanzi, Dartmouth President John Kemeny (himself a regular bedtime reader of Howe's mystery books), President Lewis Bressett of the Hanover Improvement Society, and Chair of the Selectmen Edward Brown. President Kemeny told the public assembled that "the celebration today is to congratulate ourselves that we live in a town that really cares." Lou Bressett announced the Improvement Society's gift of $10,000 to the building fund.

Both Maurice Aldrich and James W. Campion III, next Chair of the Selectboard, were concerned about space for future library expansion. Through their negotiations with Roscoe and Mollie Nichols, it was arranged that the Corporation would purchase the Nichols property next door to the Howe site. Roscoe and Mollie, both in their eighties, were to hold the 20-year mortgage and live there as long as they wished.

Library life in the interim

Meanwhile in 1974, Library life went on. Howe placed book racks in many community locations (waiting rooms, barber shops, etc.) and stocked them with 1,200 paperbacks that had been gifts to the Library. These Pick-a-Paperback collections were rotated and replenished once a month—a new form of community outreach for Howe.

That same year the state granted $3,253 to Howe as a consequence of its status as a Service Center Library in the statewide system. This money was used to purchase books in anticipation of the expanded shelving capacity in the new building. Book prices in the mid-seventies were escalating at about 15% each year. All libraries were relying more heavily on interlibrary loan through the statewide system.

The Children's Room acquired its first cassette tape/picture book sets, along with some sturdy cloth or board books especially for toddlers. Children's librarian Pegge Strickler was increasingly focusing on pre-schoolers, with story hours, group visits from nursery schools and day care centers, and advisory work with smaller libraries just developing preschool collections.

Mary Ann Rupert, an experienced librarian, began working at Howe for a few hours each week. She was the only other trained

PHOTO BY ROWLAND B. REEVE

COURTESY OF DARTMOUTH COLLEGE LIBRARY

Gus and Kate Tuckerman converse in the reading room, circa 1974. Photos above and on following page by Dartmouth student Rowland B. Reeve for his "Visual Ethnography of the Howe Library" paper.

Two "regulars" absorbed in the morning papers, circa 1974

professional on the staff and was especially valued for her reference abilities.

In spring Patti Eckels was named New Hampshire Librarian of the Year for her contributions to both statewide and community library services. The Librarian of the Year had actually spent much of her year crawling about on the floors of successful new library buildings in other towns, with tape measure in hand and eyes open for innovative ideas that might be borrowed.

Former Librarian Grace Kingsland died at the age of 97 and left her estate to Howe Library. Until a short time before her death she was still an avid reader, enjoying the stacks of books regularly delivered to her apartment. Her frugality was legend but no one had dreamed she would have $25,000 to bequeath to Howe.

At the annual Corporation meeting near the beginning of 1975, the Librarian's report paid this tribute to the indefatigable Posey Fowler, whose energy and commitment had spearheaded the movement toward a new building from the beginning:

"Mrs. Fowler will be telling you more about the work of the Building Committee. What I'm sure she won't tell you is the

extent of her contribution to this whole undertaking. Wearing the three hats of President of the Board, Chair of the Building Committee and Chief Fund Raiser has demanded 8 day weeks, sleepless nights and a vacationless summer. A recent newspaper picture showed her wearing still another hat, a construction worker's helmet. I hope that picture was for publicity purposes only and that she won't have to become part of Trumbull Nelson's crew. But of one thing I am certain, after watching her this year—if it's necessary, she'll not only learn to swing a hammer, she'll swing it vigorously and expertly."

That report also gave thanks to Genevieve Steele and Ruth Smead, as it had for many years. Mrs. Steele each year worked wonders with her clever fingers and artistic eye, arranging flowers brought in by some of Hanover's greenest thumbs (such as Frederick Page and Manning Moody) or bringing them from her own garden. There were almost always eye-catching arrangements on the hall table, even in the middle of winter, when Mrs. Steele would walk over from her house around the corner, ski pole in hand if it were icy, often with flowers purchased for Howe by the Garden Club, or evergreens and something bright to accent them.

Ruth Smead's craftsmanship in book mending was really too elegant to be termed "mending." She reconstructed many books that would otherwise have had to be sent away to the bindery. When she could no longer come to the Library to do this, Patti Eckels delivered stacks of them to her home and picked them up when their pages and binding were ready to resume active duty.

Both Mrs. Steele and Mrs. Smead were far from young but they generously shared their talents and energy with the Library, and somehow made the staff feel that it was a favor to these two women to allow them to be useful.

At that same Board meeting, Patti had to report that Hanover, like other towns in the state, was having fiscal problems because of inflation and decreased revenues, forcing budget cuts for all departments. All discretionary expenses, such as travel to conferences or funds for new equipment, had been eliminated, but it was still necessary to make a major cut in either staff or book budget. She chose to cut the staff budget, feeling that it would do less permanent damage to the Library. As a result, the Library would be closed every Thursday. What no one foresaw, and what Patti had to report at the end of that year, was that

> *"Library use did not decline; in fact it continued to increase as it had been doing, and the circulation desk staff were put in the exhausting and unfair position of coping with more business in a five-day week than they had in a six-day week."*

At the end of January 1975 Neal Berlin resigned as Town Manager to become manager of Iowa City. His departure was viewed with great regret by the town in general and certainly by those connected with Howe, who knew how lucky the Library had been to have his help in bridging the years from totally private to public/private existence, and in planning for the new building. Sadly, his successor took little interest in the Library.

By-laws were revised in 1975, with a view to the new Town status of Howe. Right-to-Know laws would now apply to Board meetings. Although one elected Board member of the Town library in Etna would serve on Howe's Board, along with a Selectman, the Corporation and Board structure would be kept intact, with the Corporation owning the new building and paying rent of $1.00 per year to the Town for the use of the land. It was agreed that the Howe Library Corporation, as a private body, was much more likely to receive future gifts and bequests than was a municipality.

In February Posey Fowler reported that construction was one-third complete and the fund-raising goal within sight. And in May the Board accepted the $140,000 offer of the American Universities Field Staff for the building at 4 West Wheelock Street. The AUFS agreed to a preservation clause and to giving the Town first refusal if it decided to sell.

During the year the Library staff was busy planning for both the new building and the move. Patti Eckels met frequently with the architects and the building committee to finalize plans for the interior and its furnishings. When the architects reported that costs were going to run considerably above estimates Howe was asked to

PHOTO BY LARRY McDONALD FOR THE VALLEY NEWS

COURTESY OF DARTMOUTH COLLEGE LIBRARY

Posey Fowler, with the help of construction supervisor Charles Judd (left), gives Dartmouth National Bank President Fred White the VIP tour through the construction site in January, 1975.

PHOTO BY SHEPLEY, BULFINCH RICHARDSON AND ABBOTT

COURTESY OF DARTMOUTH COLLEGE LIBRARY

New building under construction, 1975

PHOTO BY SHEPLEY, BULFINCH RICHARDSON AND ABBOTT

COURTESY OF DARTMOUTH COLLEGE LIBRARY

Interior view of construction, 1975

cut back on its shelving requirements. Emerson Greenaway and Patti did some calculating, came up with a new shelving figure, and reported that the Library (which they had intended to be adequate for 20 to 25 years) would probably now be in need of more space at the end of 15 years. The architects then modified the plan by cutting 1,500 square feet, assuring the committee that their design would make future expansion an easy option.

In July, Patti and Mr. Greenaway spent one day visiting the exhibits of the furnishings and equipment vendors at the annual conference of the American Library Association. They came away with many ideas and prices, but Patti also learned she had been touring the conference with "Mr. Library" himself. Everywhere they went, people stopped Emerson for a hug, a handshake, a joyful reunion. This wise and kind man with the twinkling eyes, for whom the staff had developed great admiration and fondness, was equally well regarded by all the library professionals and salespeople who had known him over his long and illustrious career.

A "home-made" moving plan

Before what was thought of as THE MOVE actually began, reference librarian Mary Ann Rupert and Patti spent many evening and weekend hours numbering and color-coding the shelves in both the old and the new buildings. They also marked off groups of books in the old building at 23-inch intervals. They had collected from local grocery stores hundreds of boxes, each just large enough to hold the 23 inches of books destined for a shelf in the new building. It would then be possible for any volunteer at the old building to remove and pack the books from any shelf, affix the shelf's colored and numbered sticker to the box, and carry the box to the moving van.

If all went according to plan, any volunteer at the new building should then be able to carry the box from the van to its exact spot in the new Library and unpack the box onto its designated shelf. After that the professional movers would deal with whatever furnishings, files, etc. were being moved. Since this was their "homemade" recipe for moving a library, Mary Ann and Patti hoped mightily that all would go well.

Howe Library closed its doors to the public at the original site at five o'clock on Saturday, November 29, 1975. On Monday, December 1, a team of 50 students from the Frances Richmond Middle School packed up 7,000 children's books, carried them to the Hanover Transfer van, then unloaded them from the van and carried them into the new building, where they stocked the shelves in the children's room.

The following day, December 2, adult and high school student volunteers moved the adult collection of 25,000 books in the same way. It couldn't have gone more smoothly. To everyone's amazement every book in the Library had found a new home by noon on Tuesday. Volunteers were treated with homemade cookies and heartfelt praise. And the best part was that many of them expressed the wish that there were a library to move every week—or some similar project where young and old could all pitch in and work together with such satisfaction.

Between November 29 and the grand opening on December 8 staff members worked from early morning to late night for eight straight days, transferring the card catalog from old drawers to new, getting the work areas organized, "reading" the shelves to be certain all the books had arrived in the proper order, and preparing the Library to be "thrown open to the public." This time the first borrower was not "young Grace Poole" by chance but, by intention, former Librarian Dorothy Hurlbutt.

PHOTO BY SHEPLEY, BULFINCH RICHARDSON AND ABBOTT

COURTESY OF DARTMOUTH COLLEGE LIBRARY

Ribbon-cutting before the doors are "thrown open to the public," December 8, 1975. Long-time staffer Mary Churchill cuts the ribbon. Trustee Ruth Young hands her the scissors.

PHOTO BY SHEPLEY, BULFINCH RICHARDSON AND ABBOTT

COURTESY OF DARTMOUTH COLLEGE LIBRARY

Former Librarian Dorothy Hurlbutt checks out the first book on opening day, with current Librarian Patricia Eckels doing the honors.

PHOTO BY SHEPLEY, BULFINCH RICHARDSON AND ABBOTT

COURTESY OF DARTMOUTH COLLEGE LIBRARY

Interior view of the new Library, from northwest corner of building

PHOTO BY SHEPLEY, BULFINCH RICHARDSON AND ABBOTT

COURTESY OF DARTMOUTH COLLEGE LIBRARY

Exterior of the new Library

Trustee Posey Piane Fowler, a native of Hanover, presided at the brief ceremony on that bright, brisk winter morning. Mary Churchill, by then a staff member for 26 years, cut the ribbon. Librarian Patricia Eckels checked out the first book to Miss Hurlbutt who was, like Mrs. Fowler, a native Hanoverian. And the public and the press poured in to look over this new Library, described later by the *Valley News* as a "beautiful, impressive facility" and "one where you can put up your feet and relax."

"The same old ladies to help you"

The facility contained two meeting rooms to house public meetings and Library programs; a comfortable reading room (with fireplace) where the magazines and newspapers were kept; spacious stack areas whose bottom and top shelves were left empty for future growth; two stereo players with headphones, where patrons could listen to recordings; many comfortable lounge chairs as well as ample study tables and chairs; a real reference section; an inviting children's room where all the shelves were truly reachable by the children; and—at last—adequate work space for the staff, and four public restrooms, none of them reached by walking through the Librarian's office. The family portraits (Emily Howe, her brother Charles, and her sister Sarah) seemed right at home in the Aldrich Room.

Library hours were shortened for the rest of the month so that staff could finish the details of settling in. But, in spite of this and the fact that December had always been the slowest month of the year, the December circulation was the highest of any monthly circulation in the history of the Library: 2,453 items. The building and equipment had cost nearly a million dollars and, although Town taxpayers had obtained a loan to help meet this cost, all the public

PHOTO BY SHEPLEY, BULFINCH RICHARDSON AND ABBOTT

COURTESY OF DARTMOUTH COLLEGE LIBRARY

The children's room in the new building, Decembr, 1975

funds were eventually repaid by the Library Corporation, thanks to the generosity of Library supporters. Everyone—even the skeptics—seemed to love Howe's new home. And some things had not changed; as one little girl enthusiastically reported to her mother, describing in great detail the glories of the new Library, "They've got everything new—but, you know, they've got the same old ladies to help you."

SEVEN

A Whole New Library World

1976 – 1981

In May of 1976 the building was officially dedicated. Dr. Ralph Hunter, born and raised in Hanover and a life-long Howe Library user, was the featured speaker.[3] In recognition of her efforts as chair of the building committee, the Board gave Posey Fowler a large photograph of the new Library. And, so that the old building would not be forgotten in all the excitement over the new one, Anne Mellor's watercolor of the West Wheelock Street building was purchased and hung in a prominent spot near the elevator. In a final tribute, the New Hampshire Library Trustees Association chose Posey and Maurice Aldrich to share the Trustee of the Year award that spring.

Dramatic increase in activity

During their first years in this new building the staff often felt they had been transported abruptly by time machine from one era to another. Compensating for the challenges of staffing

3. Ralph Hunter's father had been the contractor for construction of the brick book stack annex at the Wheelock Street building in 1914.

NEW HOWE LIBRARY BUILDING

DEDICATION PROGRAM

SUNDAY, MAY 23, 1976

WELCOME

Mrs. Richard Fowler, *Chairman*

The Howe Library Board of Trustees

INTRODUCTION OF SPECIAL GUESTS AND FRIENDS

REMARKS

James Ford Clapp, Jr., *Partner,*

Shepley, Bulfinch Richardson & Abbott

COMMENTS

Mrs. Fowler

GUEST SPEAKER

Dr. Ralph Hunter

TEA

Program for formal dedication of the new Library, May 23, 1976

and supervising this vastly larger building and meeting the increased demand for service was the excitement of being able to participate fully, at last, in a new era of public library growth and change. Throughout the country libraries were drawing in new patrons with programs and services not previously offered; with its new spaciousness, Howe could be part of this whole new library world.

In-house listening equipment for the rapidly growing collection of records and tapes was a particularly popular new service. One elderly patron came in nearly every morning to enjoy his favorite classical records from a comfortable chair near a window, and in the late afternoon teenagers used the record and tape players for their own quite different music.

The children's room also offered listening equipment for records and tapes, as well as viewing equipment for filmstrips. In that area, corkboard panels provided a perfect showplace for artwork, stories, and poems produced by the children of the community. The roomy, comfortable picture book section attracted many contented-looking children, snuggling with a parent while reading a favorite story or perhaps putting together a jigsaw puzzle. But the biggest new attraction was undoubtedly the large aquarium, where small children pressed their noses to the glass to watch the colorful tropical fish perform. The children's curiosity led Pegge Strickler to do a good bit of research on the exotic creatures, and she soon began referring to herself as "the resident ichthyologist."

Since Howe now owned a microfilm reader, David Hewitt, editor and publisher of the *Hanover Gazette* and always a good friend and supporter of the Library, donated the complete microfilmed *Gazette* back to 1885. Other microfilmed newspapers and many magazines were soon added. Dave Hewitt's death later that first year was a significant loss, both to the Library and to the community he had loved and served so well.

With the addition of 38 weekly hours of staff time in 1976, Mary Soderberg and Elizabeth Slive joined the staff as part-time circulation assistants. These extra staff hours, the enlarged space, and a budget that allowed Howe to again be open six days a week made possible the improvement of existing services as well as the addition of the new ones.

Interlibrary loan traffic increased significantly, as did reference services, thanks to the presence of Mary Ann Rupert during the busiest hours. And, with adequate space to showcase the 100-plus magazines and the fast-growing book collection, circulation grew by 28% the first year. Many of these borrowers were first-time users, a good portion of them drawn in by community use of the meeting rooms or attendance at the Library's weekly programs.

Meeting rooms: a significant addition

The two multi-purpose meeting rooms, available not only for Library use but for the programs of other non-profit organizations, were perhaps the most significant new addition; during that first year they were used on 189 occasions by 56 different groups. The larger room, named for Betty Mayer, who had seen this community need and provided the funding, seated a hundred people and came equipped with a projection booth for showing films, a piano for musical events, and comfortable furniture which could be arranged to suit various needs. The smaller room, given by Frances McCann Murray in memory of her late husband, banker and community leader Elden Murray, was equally useful for smaller meetings and for children's storytimes and craft sessions.

The Mayer and Murray Rooms enabled Howe to present adult programs for the first time, and to greatly expand children's programming. For the children, in addition to the traditional storytimes and the weekly films, Pegge Strickler began to include all sorts of programs—talks by area authors and illustrators of children's books, performances by mimes and magicians, plays and puppet shows. After tackling a woodworking course, Pegge built her own puppet stage and took up puppetry. And, during that first year in the new building, she arranged for 37 different school and youth groups, from preschoolers to middle schoolers, to visit Howe, learn about the Library's resources and hear book talks.

For the adults, Thursday became Howe Library day, with adult programs planned for the Mayer Room each Thursday afternoon or evening. There were prose and poetry readings, book discussions, lectures, slide talks, films, and concerts, always accompanied by monthly art, photo, or craft exhibits showcasing local talent. Each exhibit opened with a meet-the-artist reception, with volunteers hostessing and providing refreshments. The community quickly came to see the new Howe as a place to share hobbies, interests and talents with others – much as the old building had been in its early years, before it became over-crowded. Soon people were volunteering their neighbors, their friends, their spouses, and even themselves as program and exhibit resources.

The programs that emerged in the early years as a result of the brainstorming and recruiting efforts of the first program planning committee offered something for everyone. Chrysanthi Bien, Betty MacDonald, Barbara Morin, Joan Snell, and Priscilla Weismann helped set the tone for all the programming throughout the remainder of Patti Eckels' tenure at Howe. The following sampling will give the flavor of their efforts; the names of the presenters will be quite familiar to old Hanover hands.

Chauncy (Chintz) Allen	*Stamp Collecting*
Lillian Bailey	*Historic Sites Outside the Village*
Peter Bien, Bill Cook, Jim Tatum	*Poetry Read to Music*
Nardi Campion	*Mother Ann of the Shakers*
Jane Chivers	*Local Ski Films of the Thirties and Forties*
Laurence Davies	*Reading from Dylan Thomas*
Bob Guest	*Equality and the Japanese Woman*
Elaine Harp & Martin Segal	*Murder, Mayhem, and Related Joys*
Elmer Harp	*Eskimo Art*
Al Ives	*Readings from Abraham Lincoln*

Bob Jaccaud	*Tracing Your Family History*
Will Lange	*Yankee Characters I Have Known*
Dr. Lou Matthews	*Your Lifestyle and Your Health*
Leonard Morrissey, Sr.	*Slide Talk, Travels in Ireland*
Frances McCann Murray	*Showing her husband Elden's travel films*
Jay Parini	*Discussing his new novel*
Jay Pierson & his son Jeff	*Across the Country by Bike*
Noel Perrin	*Books and Non-Books*
Robin Robinson	*Slide talk, Travels in Greece*
Peter Saccio	*Shakespeare's Kings*
Carolyn Steiner	*A directed reading of Eliot's "Cocktail Party"*
Walker Weed	*Telling Treasures From Turkeys*
Henry Williams	*Japanese Theatre*
Rebecca Williams	*Slide talk, Japanese crafts*

Some of the diverse exhibits in those first years include Deborah Crowell's wildflower photographs; Ruth Malmstrom's Scandinavian knitting; Basil Milavsoroff's wonderful, whimsical folk puppets; original book illustrations by Trina Schart Hyman; the work of the Upper Valley Weavers; Diane Haas' quilted creations; and Josephine Wolfenden's paintings.

Musical events included regular concerts by the Women's Chorus, directed by Joan Snell, which met weekly at Howe; the Young Musicians series, spotlighting groups of high school instrumentalists; and numerous recitals by individual soloists.

Remarkably all the participants, many of them college faculty, volunteered their time. This was a blessing because, although the Librarian and her volunteer committee had big ideas, they had no programming budget.

DESIGN BY DIANE HAAS

Brochure and logo by Diane Haas containing information on Howe history, services, and layout of the new building

To keep the public informed about all this new activity, circulation supervisor Diane Haas designed and edited a monthly publication called *Here's Howe,* which provided a calendar of programs plus news about books, events, and people on the Library scene. Diane continued producing book displays and eye-catching posters and designed a brochure, funded with a gift to the Corporation, which included a brief history of the Library, a floor plan, and information about Howe services and programs. This was available at the desk and answered many of the questions asked by visitors who came to see this new facility. Howe Library had become part of the tour (Baker Library, Hopkins Center, covered bridges, etc.) on which Hanoverians took their visiting friends and relatives.

Volunteers help make it possible

How did a small staff find the time to deal with this dramatic increase in Library activity? They couldn't possibly have managed it without the help of many, many volunteers. In that first year, 47

Library users responded to the Library's call for help and were trained to assist at the circulation desk, process new books, help with an inventory, and perform other assorted tasks. Ranging in age from a retired lawyer to a young woman with a full-time job and expecting her first child, the volunteers were a varied and delightful group who often caused staff to take a fresh look at how they were doing things. The director of the Retired Senior Volunteer Program reported that the Library had a reputation among her volunteers as "a very nice place to work, but you really have to be good."

PHOTO BY ADRIAN BOUCHARD

Hanover town quilt, created in 1976 by 22 local needlewomen to hang behind the circulation desk.

Work on the Hanover town quilt occupied another group of volunteers during the country's bicentennial year. Diane Haas invited women of the community to design and create quilt squares highlighting Hanover places, institutions, and events. Experienced quilters and novices took up the challenge, each hand-sewing a square, or squares, of her own design. The results were inventively detailed scenes of life in Hanover and Etna, and Howe proudly displayed the quilt on the wall behind the circulation desk where it hung for many years.[4]

When the annual architectural issue of *Library Journal* arrived that December, all involved with the Library were proud and pleased to find Howe featured in an article on the nation's newest public library buildings, complete with construction data and photographs.

A comparison of Library statistics from 1966 and 1976 shows that during that ten-year period the Library's annual circulation had grown from 78,555 to 131,744; registered borrowers had increased from 2,601 to 5,938; and the annual budget had burgeoned from $32,408 to $117,044. Howe had certainly become the community center planners envisioned, and by the end of 1976 people were beginning to request Sunday hours.

In February of 1977 the Library began opening Sunday afternoons, operating with just one staff member and two trained high school students and, of necessity, offering limited reference service. The first Sunday 110 people took advantage of these extra hours. Having a welcoming fire blazing in the fireplace was a pleasant "extra" for those who settled down to read the Sunday papers—once staff members learned to light the fire without setting off the smoke detectors and bringing the fire department noisily to the rescue.

That year Diane and Patti developed a 37-page cross-referenced manual for the circulation desk volunteers, prompting one

4. Late in the century the quilt, growing fragile from years of sunlight and dust, was taken down to protect it from further damage. In 2001, a generous gift funded its restoration at the American History Textile Museum. It now hangs, protectively framed, in the Aldrich Room.

volunteer to remark that "this would be a real eye-opener for anyone who still thinks all you need to know to work in a library is how to hold a rubber stamp." Forty volunteers gave 3,534 hours in 1977, almost the equivalent of two full-time employees. In appreciation the staff prepared and served the first annual volunteer luncheon, a tradition that has continued to the present day.

But the euphoria about all the good fortune the Library was enjoying was somewhat dampened when a series of break-ins occurred. Minor thefts—some petty cash, a small clock—were indicating "visitors," who usually seemed to come late on Sundays. Staff began locking away cash, stamps, etc., at closing time, but still there was evidence of trespassing. The worst fear was that when the visitors found nothing to steal they might turn to vandalism and some morning thousands of catalog cards might be found scattered on the floor.

After months of anxiety the Board had an intrusion alarm system installed, and within two weeks the police had apprehended two juvenile culprits. But, for the staff, the months preceding that arrest were a nightmare. Because the contractor declared the outside locks foolproof, it was assumed that staff carelessness with the keys or in locking up had to be the problem; lock-up procedures became more and more complex and all the locks were re-keyed. When the boys were finally caught staff members felt vindicated. The locks had been *intended* to be foolproof, but some of the door frames had settled so that the locks were out of alignment, and the boys had been jimmying one with a pen-knife.

On a happier note, private gifts and volunteerism continued to make it possible for the Library to offer "extras." James Wicker had specified that $5,000 of his large gift to the building fund should be invested, with income dedicated to a Librarian's Discretionary

Fund. This income, about $450 per year, allowed for all sorts of innovations that would have been hard to get into the budget. Its first use was to purchase materials to construct the handsome wood and glass display case near the front entry, which was designed and built by volunteer craftsman Harry Cooke. In succeeding years the Librarian used the fund as seed money for a variety of new services, including a framed collection of circulating art reproductions and photographs.

Harry Cooke's wife, Thelma, a skilled Braille transcriber, began meeting weekly at Howe to pass along this art to 21 volunteers from 11 towns. Their purpose was to supply the need of any New Hampshire resident for individualized Braille material for school or work, and the group continued for several years.

The Elden Murray Photo Contest, still an annual event today, was first sponsored by the Library's Elden Murray Fund in 1977. Planned and judged by a volunteer committee, the contest attracted 260 entries that first year, and has continued through the years both to challenge photographers and to reward those viewers who come to see the exhibit.

Barbara Hayward, for whom the children's terrace was named, provided tubs for that area and had them planted with bright geraniums each summer. The Hanover Garden Club agreed to care for the shrubs on the grounds and contributed redwood tubs for flowering plants near the front entrance.

Garden Club members also continued the tradition of supplying and arranging fresh flowers inside the Library. Genevieve Steele had asked to retire from her long commitment to this job. "The scale of the new building is so different," she explained. "My little arrangements would get lost and since I was asked to do this job for two years, which somehow stretched to thirteen, perhaps I deserve a vacation?" Pam Doenges and Elizabeth Tobiasson, assisted by other gardeners, took over this assignment in 1976 and are still responsible, 24 years later, for the colorful seasonal bouquets.

In December of 1977 Pegge Strickler began a tradition of festive winter holiday celebrations in the children's room, enlivened by young musicians and singers from the schools and made appealing by those who made or loaned special Christmas or Hanukkah decorations. For years Walker and Hazel Weed cut and brought in a Christmas tree, and there was always a tree on the children's terrace with food for the birds.

Also that December, but not in a holiday spirit, the Board was alarmed when two Selectmen suggested Howe Library should charge a 'user fee' to townspeople to help with expenses. Public Libraries, as long made clear by New Hampshire law, are of course prohibited from doing this. That winter also marked the first of the continuing complaints about a parking shortage, a problem that remained unsolved a quarter century later.

Meeting community needs

At the Corporation meeting in January of 1978, two notable Trustees were honored. Retiring Trustee Jack Stebbins was cited for his 23 years of wise and forward-looking service and Maurice Aldrich, who had been killed in an auto accident the previous month, was praised for his long devotion to and financial care of the Library: "Howe Library has lost a devoted friend, but his spirit will be felt in the Library for years to come."

Shortly before his death Mr. Aldrich had had the satisfaction of announcing that paid-up pledges for the new building now totaled $246,914, from approximately 500 contributors. To Leonard Morrissey, Jr., then elected Treasurer, fell the task of reviewing and making order of the vast number of boxes containing the careful financial records Mr. Aldrich had accumulated in his 32-year tenure.

That year, concerned about the costs of debt service on the Library's construction loan, the Trustees extended the term of the construction loan to twenty years, so that interest payments would be closer to endowment income. All unrestricted income was pledged to reimburse the Town for debt service until the loan was repaid. The Board also raised the annual non-resident fee to $25 per family unit, roughly equivalent to the per-family cost to Hanover taxpayers. At that time there were 340 non-resident units.

Staff efforts in 1978 focused heavily on improving reference services. Although the reference librarian was now on-site 25 hours a week, that accounted for fewer than half the hours Howe was open. Consequently time was set aside at weekly staff meetings to improve the reference skills of all public service staff. Staff members and volunteers greatly expanded the annually updated file on local and area organizations, adding information on nursery schools and day care centers (their costs, hours, programs, and staffs). Mary Ann Rupert established a Hanover municipal reference section with building codes, zoning laws, studies done by Town committees, and background information about decisions citizens would be asked to make. At the same time she developed a bibliography of inexpensive paperback reference books recommended for home collections. Howe had progressed far beyond the "trivial" reference use Frances Haslett had described.

Howe librarians invited Richmond School and Hanover High School faculties to meet with them to ascertain how all might work more closely together to meet student needs for information resources. Teachers who came to these sessions were encouraged to familiarize themselves with the scope and limitations of Howe's nonfiction and reference collections, so that they did not send students for help Howe could not provide. The new building had perhaps led some to overestimate the Library's holdings, which was frustrating for the students.

Teachers were not the only ones whose expectations of service were sometimes more than staff could match. One young mother, having heard about the new file on day care centers, phoned to ask about a rumor that there was a file listing names and phone numbers for all the baby sitters in Hanover. She was disappointed to learn that no such file had even been contemplated.

Howe was, however, still adding services. Mary Soderberg, who had decided to further her training by taking all the Public Library Techniques courses offered through the state library system, was inspired by her course on library services for teens to begin a young adult paperback section at Howe. Her thoughtful choices made this collection an instant success, and it soon grew to include hardcover books as well.

In 1978 national statistics showed that the average library had 65 hours of paid staff time for every hour of volunteer time. Given that Howe used only five hours of staff time for each volunteer hour, the Library was clearly maximizing its use of volunteers. The Librarian heard often at New England regional meetings that many library directors were reluctant to use volunteers lest the public come to believe that volunteers could supplant paid staff, but this was a gamble she chose to take. The financial benefit to Hanover taxpayers was considerable, and the fresh insights and work relief the volunteers provided were equally appreciated.

Participation in the statewide system continued to be a commitment Howe staff found worthwhile and to which they contributed as time allowed. For two years Diane Haas gave workshops on creating library displays during the annual conference of the New Hampshire Library Association. Mary Ann Rupert and Patti Eckels participated in the 1978 New Hampshire Conference on Library and Information Service, precursor of a White House conference the following year. Both led discussion groups of lay-

Elaine Harp, Trustee 1964–1977, known for her reader's notes and her horror tales of maintenance in the old building

men and librarians throughout the two-day conference. Mrs. Eckels was appointed to the newly created State Library Commission's Communication Exchange, which held monthly meetings to brief Commissioners on the needs of various sized libraries in the state.

Signs of the times

Elaine Harp's retirement from her long tenure on the Board was announced at the 1979 Corporation meeting. Mrs. Harp had played an important role in the work of the maintenance committee in the old building, with all its problems, and had often regaled the Trustees with tales of the odd situations and odder tenants she had encountered in her duties. (The apartments were then no longer reserved for bachelor professors. Many were occupied by younger people.) Trustee Tay Burnett's humorous tribute masterfully recalled for Elaine some of those encounters including this one: "I remind you of the days when one Howe apartment housed a snapping turtle, several flying squirrels, an assortment of rats, a boa constrictor, a French horn that was heard at all hours, and a life-sized cardboard cut-out of a Playboy Bunny who later became the tenant's bride."

It was in 1979 that the Board embarked on what came to be known as "the Walpole woodlot saga." This saga became the counterpart—though perhaps in a lighter vein— of the unceasing and long-unresolved search for a pension plan of earlier years, and persistently reappeared on the agenda over the years. The property had long been listed as a Corporation asset but now, with Maurice Aldrich gone, no one knew just where it was or what its value might be. (Since then evidence has been found indicating that it had been in the Hitchcock family and it probably came to Howe as part of Emily Howe's estate.) Its existence was brought to the Board's at-

DARTMOUTH COLLEGE LIBRARY

This property was the subject of the "Walpole woodlot saga."

tention when an abutting property owner complained that the Library's dead trees had fallen on his property. For the next several years meetings were periodically enlivened by reports from Peter Morrisson, who took on the task of locating the lot, tramping over it, and talking to realtors and appraisers about its possibilities. Some advised it should be logged. Others counseled it should be sold as a unit. Others argued it could be profitably sub-divided. It seemed to be a never-ending, and in Peter's telling, endlessly amusing entanglement.

In response to complaints about handicapped access, the Board that year agreed to raise the level of the sidewalk at the lower entrance, eliminating the two-inch step at the doorway. They also resolved to have the heavy double doors there rehung for easier opening but the latter proved impossible until, a few years later, automatic openers were installed at that entrance. In the meantime, at the suggestion of a young handicapped user, the Library provided a keyed doorbell at the main entrance so that staff could be summoned to assist those needing help. A few years later the front sidewalk was also regraded to level that entrance as well.

Original plans for the building had included totally handicap-accessible entrances, and it was discouraging to find, once the sidewalks were poured, a two-inch lip at each entrance. The Americans With Disabilities Act had not yet been passed, and architects and builders were not as informed or concerned as they would later have to become. But it was a sign of the times that those with disabilities no longer silently accepted barriers, but asked for and expected efforts to remove them.

Another sign of the times, reflecting the high cost of energy in the seventies, was the effort to conserve electricity and heating oil. The Board and Town agreed to ask for an energy audit of the building. Considering the vast areas of glass and the very high ceiling, the building was generally found to be more efficient than expected, but in 1979 some insulation was added, glass doors were placed on the fireplace, and energy-saving light bulbs were installed. These were the years when many homeowners in northern New England were purchasing window quilts, heating their houses with wood stoves, and wearing several layers of clothing inside in winter. Window quilts for the Library would no doubt have made a vast difference in Howe's energy bills, but the payback time was considered too long to make this a good investment.

Gifts to enhance the book and magazine collections had been increasing rapidly since the move. In 1979 individuals and organi-

The Howe Library

HANOVER, NEW HAMPSHIRE

This volume has been purchased from a fund that was created by EDWARD CONNERY LATHEM & ELIZABETH FRENCH LATHEM

HANOVER . Conservation COUNCIL

zations gave the funds to purchase 686 books as well as 40 of the 179 magazine subscriptions. Many were memorial books, but a new idea originated that year when Dr. Raymond Jackson decided to honor his wife Alice on Mother's Day with a gift to the book fund. The idea was picked up by another husband, who saw the inscribed bookplate and did the same for his wife at Christmas. Soon Howe was receiving gifts to the book fund in honor of birthdays, anniversaries, and other special occasions and began actively promoting the idea by supplying appropriate forms at the circulation desk.

A Lions Club gift of $1,000 in memory of Bill Griffiths specified that the income from the fund be designated to increase Howe's collection of large-print books for those with failing vision. Other organizations that had long made annual gifts for books and magazines in their fields of interest, notably the Conservation Council and the Garden Club, increased those gifts as the Library became more heavily used.

The Library staff continued to hone their skills and to develop new ideas. Six staff members attended workshops or took courses in 1979, and Mary Soderberg completed the last of the eight courses in Public Library Techniques she'd begun four years earlier. Pegge Strickler initiated an annual bookmark contest for children, with the winning entries in various age groups printed and available at the circulation desk. And several staff members became involved with the new summer Street Fest in Hanover.

They set up a booth at the Street Fest to sell discarded books, pass out flyers advertising Library services, and display some of the Library's more unusual wares. After high winds nearly demolished the booth before the celebration had even begun, the staff began exploring all-weather booth design. In 1980 their structure was more durable, and the Street Fest became an annual part of the Library's community outreach.

Mary Churchill attained another milestone in her long career at Howe in June of 1979. The staff gave a 30th anniversary picnic lunch in her honor, and Town Manager Peter Gartland presented her with a Dartmouth rocking chair. Luckily, although she was pleased with the chair, Mary was not ready to retire to it.

In 1980, when circulation assistant Holly Porter (who had replaced Liz Slive a few years earlier) resigned because of illness, Peggy Hyde took her place, beginning a long and notable career at Howe. Peggy had come aboard as a circulation desk volunteer soon after the building opened and had quickly graduated to the role of paid substitute. Now, along with her circulation duties, she began to work on topical book displays and to share with Mary Soderberg the responsibility for adding to the young adult collection as the enthusiasm for that collection grew.

The meeting rooms had continued to grow in popularity. In 1980 they were used 533 times by 113 different non-profit organizations, ranging from such community fixtures as the League of Women Voters and the Historical Society to such new groups as the Childbirth Educators of the Upper Valley and the Beekeepers Association. This meant that usage of the rooms had nearly tripled in the four years they had been available and the number of organizations served had doubled. Grateful for the space, the groups were consistently considerate in leaving the rooms in good condition, and several of the larger groups began making annual contributions in appreciation. In accordance with the donors' original intentions, and despite occasional urging from the Selectmen, the rooms remained available free of charge.

Howe measures itself

In 1981 the Library elected to participate in the Planning Process designed by the American Library Association. The ALA's goal for this process was to replace the old national guidelines (so many square feet of space per user, so many volumes per capita, etc.) by helping a library set its own goals based on local needs. Using materials developed by the ALA, each participating library would do a self-study.

Having completed five years in their new quarters, Patti Eckels and reference librarian Mary Ann Rupert were eager to learn, through an objective study, whether the Library was moving in the directions really desired by Hanover's residents. In addition, Patti had been working with a committee charged with recommending a plan to restructure the statewide library system and knew that the State Library was eager to see a New Hampshire library carry out a pilot self-study. With the encouragement of the Board, Mary Ann and Patti recruited nine members of the community and two Trustees, including President Mary Ann Harris, to join them in forming a committee and proceeding with the Planning Process.

The committee created several different questionnaires and 35 volunteers helped administer written and telephone surveys of more than 900 people from various age groups, both Library users and non-users. At the end of the process Mary Ann Rupert took on the formidable job of pulling all the statistics together. The results were both rewarding and useful.

The committee learned that Howe was an exceptionally active library: 74% of the adults contacted in the telephone survey had used the Library in the past six months, compared with 51% in a national study. And 61% of Hanover adults visited the Library at least once a month, compared with a national average of 20%.

According to the survey, the level of satisfaction with Howe's policies and services was high (94.6%) but there were still unmet needs in both print and non-print collections, and it was clear Howe needed to find cost-effective ways to increase awareness of many of its newer services and programs. The community also wanted to be assured of maximum coordination of library services between Howe and the other local and regional libraries. Based on its findings, the planning committee submitted detailed recommendations to the Board in October of 1981.

Pegge Strickler's first annual children's poetry contest attracted over 300 entries. Howe published many of these in a booklet, and some also appeared in the *Valley News*. Pegge, who by that time had been children's librarian for ten years, was rightly viewed as an expert in children's literature, and was consulted by the Upper Valley Teacher Training Program and children's literature students at both the college and the high school.

That year another ten-year veteran, Diane Haas, left the staff. Diane, who had been in charge of the circulation desk and had designed and edited most of the Library's publications, had brought great vitality and creative talent to Howe. Polly Gould, a professional librarian and new part-time staff member, replaced Diane as head of circulation and brought new strengths to that position. Peggy Hyde expertly took over much of Diane's work in graphic design and arranging exhibits.

EIGHT

Evolving Role of the Library

1982 – 1984

Financial challenges again

PETER GARTLAND, who had replaced John Stinson as Town Manager in 1978, had forewarned department heads in late 1981 that the next fiscal year would be difficult because of decreased revenue from the State to the Town, and indeed it was. Though each department had prepared a frugal budget, they were asked to make further savings. With inflation rates running high, these were difficult times for public service providers at all government levels. State and town governments, unlike the federal government, could not just plunge into debt to make ends meet.

Howe made its required cuts in 1982 by eliminating Friday evening and Sunday afternoon hours, removing children's programs from the budget, reducing the book budget by $3,400, and raising the annual non-resident fee to $35.

Now that there was actually space to expand the collection, the book budget reduction was hard to accept, but it was done to protect an equal amount, already requested and approved, for adding 20 more staff hours. Staff morale had reached a dangerous low, as increases in staff had not kept pace with the increased demand for services in this larger facility. All staff members were putting in extra unpaid hours in a fruitless effort to stay on top of the workload.

Many people feel that librarians have "cushy" jobs. Even those who regularly express appreciation for the level of service they find at Howe probably have no idea of the amount of behind-the-scenes work required or the stress caused by too few people trying to do too much—and always with a smile. Results of a New Hampshire study of medium-sized public libraries that year confirmed what the Librarian had already suspected: though Howe's cost per circulation was average, its circulation-per-staff ratio was one-third higher than average and its circulations-per-book ratio one-fourth higher. Both books and staff were working harder than in the average library of comparable size, and the extra labor was taking its toll on both the staff and the collection.

With public funding strained, the Library was fortunate to have an exceptionally good year in private giving. An anonymous donor provided $10,000 earmarked for a fund to support maintenance of the Mayer Room furnishings. Jean Witherell left Howe half her estate, over $55,000. And the warm response to appeals for private donations to offset the reduced book budget replaced nearly all that had been cut.

Howe became one of the Talking Books centers for the State Library. It was also awarded a federal grant, in conjunction with Dartmouth's Dana Biomedical Library, to purchase books on health and medical care geared to the general reader. Five new sections of shelving were added for non-fiction.

Considering how to make Corporation membership more active and meaningful, the Trustees decided to offer an orientation session each year for newly elected members to familiarize them with both the Library and the role of the Corporation. They also decided to begin taking attendance at the annual meeting and to offer emeritus status to older members who maintained their interest in Howe but did not wish to be actively involved.

To implement the Planning Process recommendations, the staff prepared a timetable for addressing each specific item. One of the goals targeted for 1982 was to increase community awareness of services the Library offered beyond book-borrowing. To this end new approaches in public relations were devised.

A newsletter, *Howe Now*, funded by the Corporation and edited by Trustee and former *Dartmouth Alumni Magazine* editor Charles Widmayer, was mailed to all Hanover homes that winter. Charlie's professional skill and his wealth of knowledge of the com-

PHOTO BY STUART BRATESMAN, JR.

Records from Howe's large collection could be enjoyed on the Library's players or borrowed for home use.

munity, along with his common sense and good humor, were of great value to the Library.

Staff also explored ways to use local broadcast media more effectively, with interview appearances and more public service announcements. In addition, several local businesses agreed to sponsor newspaper ads listing Howe's schedule of monthly programs. And a new directory on the main floor guided users to specific areas and highlighted lesser known services.

Other recommendations implemented that year involved specific areas of the collection where users had wished for improvement: more books on tape were purchased; music tapes were added to the collection; some specific subject fields (music, theatre, home decoration photography, sports) received a larger share of the budget allocation; and staff established a regular schedule for up-dating travel guides.

A third goal was to enhance cooperation with other libraries. Howe and the Lebanon Public Library initiated direct interlibrary loan service between the two libraries for new books and for all fiction, short-cutting the State Library's slower ILL process. In addition, the reference librarian made visits to school and college libraries, gaining a better understanding of the scope of their reference collections so that she could make more useful referrals.

That summer Howe welcomed back children's librarian Pegge Strickler. Pegge had been on leave from January through June, working with her husband in a refugee resettlement camp in Thailand for six months, teaching English as a second language.

During her absence Mary Soderberg conducted the weekly story hours and covered the children's desk during many busy hours. Just before Pegge's return, Lurlene Cole came to Howe as Technical Services Assistant, replacing five-year staff member Eniko Gellai, whose family moved from Hanover.

Also in 1982, the Hanover Improvement Society offered Howe the 69" by 167" mural being removed in the Nugget Theater remodeling. Would the Library be willing to lease and display it for ninety-nine years for one dollar? Patti Eckels suggested the Elden Murray Room as a fine location for this bit of Hanover history; the Board agreed and she sent the mural out to be framed.

When it was returned, to her chagrin, the delivery men were unable to work the large piece around a sharp corner into the room and there was no other spot large enough. Happily, at the December Board meeting Trustees Leonard Morrissey and Peter Morrison saw this as a challenge and, surmising that the lightweight piece might be a bit flexible, they carefully maneuvered it into the room. Accustomed to thornier problems, both Trustees and Librarian had seldom felt such a sense of accomplishment for a few minutes work. In gratitude Patti promised a chocolate cake for the next meeting. Thus began the tradition of the "annual chocolate cake" which she continued to bake until her retirement, after which Trustee Ruth Young (famed for her provision of goodies at many a Library function) took over that task. "Vignette Scenes Along Main Street, Hanover, N.H." painted by Bernard F. Chapman in 1951, has hung in the Murray Room ever since.

Real estate questions

During 1983 the Trustees were heavily involved with problems that had more to do with real estate than Library services. The Walpole woodlot saga accelerated its pace when property taxes on the lot began to rise. Peter Morrison's explorations had revealed a rough, rolling terrain with very few large trees, and it began to seem wise to hire some experts. The expert hired to do an official appraisal decided there must first be an official survey; the surveyor reported a total of 34 acres but then found an error that brought the total to 41. When foresters declared its value as a logging resource was minimal, the Trustees decided to terminate these endless investigations and put the property on the market.

A more pressing concern was the future of the Nichols house to the east of the Library, purchased earlier as a possible expansion site. Roscoe Nichols, now a widower in his late eighties, had decided to move to California to be with his son. Should the Trustees rent the building, raze it, or try to move it? Roscoe's winter departure required a prompt decision, something the Board had always found difficult, preferring a prolonged and deliberate consideration. In many ways the cautious spirit of Maurice Aldrich lived on.

Three Trustees, touring the large house that winter to assess its condition, found a very cold building, with water running from the second floor to the basement. A broken gauge, registering full, had camouflaged an empty oil tank and the water pipes had frozen and burst. Pipes were drained and the exploration of options begun, but the water damage strengthened the Board's resolve not to go back into the business of renting out apartments in an old house.

In April they decided to brave public criticism and raze the house in order to provide much-needed Library parking, but in May they learned that the area was not zoned for parking. After one prospective buyer explored unsuccessfully the possibility of moving the house, the Board accepted an offer in September to lease the house for ten years, at a low annual rental, to a tenant who would take on the taxes and the extensive renovations to plumbing, heating, electrical systems, and decor. The house was nicely restored, providing a neat short-term solution.

October minutes record the Trustees' decision to invite Hanover's new Town Manager, Clifford Vermilya, to a meeting in the near future. He would not have to ask for an invitation as Neil

Berlin had thirteen years before. However, like Neil Berlin, Cliff Vermilya would prove to be a manager who understood the importance of libraries and worked to support Howe's services. He was a reader and his interest in the Library was manifest from his first day on the job.

Daily life

In the daily life of the Library, there were several happy events in 1983. Sunday hours were restored by popular demand, as Library users could no longer envision a library not open for them on Sundays. Artist Anne Mellor designed handsome bookplates for

Bookplate designed by Anne Mellor, 1983

Howe's memorial and "honor" books, as well as a card to notify the appropriate person. The designs were given to Howe by this good Library friend, who also volunteered to hand-letter the required names as needed on individual bookplates. And a gift from long-time Trustee Barbara Morin made possible the purchase of wooden puzzles for the circulating preschool collection. There had been in-house puzzles for several years, but now children could borrow their favorites to enjoy at home.

Less pleasant was another discovery of some worrisome vandalism. Small fires were found set outside against the brick walls; two chairs in the children's room were slashed; the fire extinguisher on the lower level was discharged all over the lobby; and a box of Library books was found dumped in a nearby gully. Although the police soon apprehended the juveniles involved the staff realized again, as they had in 1976, that even in the most peaceful towns supervising a public building is not without its problems.

That year the Librarian tried to address another of the on-going challenges, dealing with the disruptive behavior of young people at Howe after school. A letter was sent to all middle and high school students, and to raise the consciousness of parents a copy was published in the *Valley News* as well.

Another round of staff musical chairs occurred in 1983. Mary Ann Rupert's resignation as reference librarian was regretfully accepted when her family moved from Hanover. Mary Ann had built Howe's reference collection and service from less-than-minimal to more-than-respectable and had provided fine reference training for other public service staff. Because there were two professionally trained librarians on staff whose families made full-time commitment difficult, the Librarian decided to experiment with job sharing. Polly Gould and Ellen Lynch began sharing supervision of both reference and circulation services, each working about two-thirds time.

Both Mary Soderberg and Peggy Hyde continued to work 25 hours a week, but each took on some additional responsibilities, passing along some of their circulation desk hours to newly hired part-time circulation assistants Charlotte Bernini and Marcia Manzo. Charlotte and Marcia had first been volunteers and then paid staff substitutes. Former volunteer Jean Watson also became a regular part-time technical services assistant.

Other staff members who had had no formal library education had followed the same progression. It was a system that worked well for Howe, as did the Librarian's willingness to have several part-time workers rather than a few full-time staff, and to allow people to move back and forth between full and part-time work to a reasonable degree. During those years Hanover was a town rich in capable young wives and mothers who had the education and initiative to become valuable staff members, provided their schedules could vary a little with their families' needs. "Fast track" is not for everyone, and it was to Howe's advantage to be adaptable.

Entering the Computer Age

In late 1983 Patti Eckels asked for and received approval to appoint a committee with computer expertise to advise the staff about purchase of a microcomputer, today called a personal computer. The plan was to use the computer both for public access—promoting computer literacy among adults—and for developing staff competence with computers.

For several years professional library journals and conferences had been full of new information about the uses of computers in libraries. Most of these uses involved automating major functions, such as circulation or cataloging. The problem for a library Howe's size was that it was too small to afford the powerful systems available at that time, and too complex to adopt the simpler, less expensive systems being used in many school libraries.

A microcomputer would not perform these major functions, but the Librarian believed it would give the staff a chance to develop its own computer skills and begin organizing some of the simpler internal operations. This experience would then equip them to plan wisely for the automation she knew was in Howe's future. Where the money would come from she did not know, but the costs were relatively modest and she hoped to find gift money to support this endeavor.

In January 1984 the committee, chaired by Trustee Lawrence Draper, was ready to begin work; by the time they had decided what equipment would work best, Patti found that recent annual gifts from AMCA Corporation and money from the Elden Murray Fund would allow for purchase of their choices. By fall Howe staff had acquired an Apple IIe, a printer, and a modem for accessing the statewide automated union catalog expected to be ready soon. They also purchased software programs for word processing, database work, and financial management, plus some additional programs for the public to experiment with (a typing tutor, an electronic spell-checker, some educational games, etc.).

After a brief introductory workshop, most of the staff taught themselves to use the hardware and the various software programs, all of which, in those days, fortunately arrived with copious written documentation. The staff worked steadily, preparing to introduce the public access project in January of 1985. By year's end staff members were regularly using the computer for word processing and were using the data base program to perform such functions as keeping the records for Howe's periodical collection. These records could be updated frequently and lists showing exact current holdings of each title could be posted for the public. They were also beginning, with volunteer help, to convert the patron registration files and the Corporation membership list into computerized data bases.

Computer projects did not absorb all the staff's time in 1984, however. Adult evening programs got off to a rousing start with "Teacher's Pet Books," wherein several outstanding teachers (Professors Bien, Cook, Perrin, and Silver from Dartmouth and Hanover High School's Eileen Kell) each took an evening to discuss some of their favorites. The community's generosity in sharing interests and talents with the Thursday audiences continued unabated.

The aquarium in the children's room, having seen the demise of too many tropical fish, became home for the flora and fauna of local ponds that year. It was expertly stocked and cared for by naturalist Sandra Miller and her son, Patchen, with various families financing this service by "adopting" the aquarium for a month at a time. This close-up lesson in pond ecology proved not only educational but also endlessly absorbing for the children.

Mary Churchill's 35 years at Howe were celebrated with a surprise party and a book fund in her honor. Since the move to the new building Mary had been supervising several volunteers who assisted with book processing and other aspects of technical services. They found her a treasure trove of information about almost any aspect of Howe Library. When they came in during their "off-duty" hours it was difficult to discourage them from taking a reference question straight to Mary, who must have wished many times for a door to close. Her patience and good humor seemed inexhaustible.

Howe continued to be active in the statewide library system. In 1984 Patti Eckels was one of two public librarians appointed to the newly created New Hampshire Automated Information Systems Board, a group of librarians from public, college, school, and hospital libraries as well as members of various state agencies. Their job was to oversee the creation and functioning of an automated statewide information network, and it was a revelation to discover the myriad details to be worked out in bringing these quite different entities together in an electronic system. New Hampshire, a small state with under-funded agencies (including the State Library), was not in the vanguard of the electronic revolution, but the State Librarian was struggling mightily to make limited resources yield optimal results.

In September of that year the Town Manager attended the Howe Board meeting to report on two projects he was asking Library staff to undertake. One was a study of the job descriptions and salary scale for Library staff as related to other Town employees, with a view to possible reclassification of positions. The other project was the future preparation of a five-to-ten-year long range plan for Library facilities, staffing, collections, and services. The Board endorsed both projects.

NINE

Pay Equity, a Party, More Planning

1985 – 1987

IN JANUARY 1985 Howe was ready to introduce the public access computer, having prepared some very brief training procedures and several pages of information about the equipment and programs. This was a self-teaching project, with users learning at their own pace as the staff had done. An appreciative public was glad to sign up in advance for time on the Apple. While many of them were simply hoping to catch up with their school-age children, others wanted to try the new technology before deciding to invest in their own equipment.

The staff gratefully welcomed the 16 additional hours for part-time circulation and technical services help that had been budgeted for the year. Little by little they felt they were gaining on the gap between the number of staff hours needed and the number the budget could handle.

Staffing and personnel issues became matters for serious study that year. Town Manager Cliff Vermilya asked Ellen Lynch to chair a committee of Town employees charged with making recommendations for revisions and clarifications in the Town personnel policy. And Mary Soderberg chaired the small staff committee he charged with examining pay equity and part-time benefits. Committee members did their research well, studying both Hanover and other comparable municipalities and documenting their findings with care.

At the end of the year all their recommendations were approved by the Town Manager and the Selectmen, with thanks for their hard work. The result was that, over a three year period, all Library positions would be moved up the classification scale at least one level, some as much as three levels, and all part-time Town employees who worked a minimum number of hours would now be entitled to benefits (except the retirement plan) on a pro-rated basis.

Since Howe had far more part-time personnel than any other department, this was a significant gain for the Library. The study attracted attention throughout the state, and Mary was later asked to speak about their work at the New Hampshire Library Association's annual conference.

Still concerned with encouraging the Corporation to play a more active role, the Board surveyed all those members who had been absent from the annual meeting for the past three years, asking whether they wished to remain active, to elect emeritus status, or to resign. Of 80 members receiving the mailing, all but 15 replied, roughly one-third choosing each option.

The ten-year mark

The "new" building would be ten years old on December 8, 1985 and was beginning to need some repairs. In 1984 all of the loft windows had been re-caulked because of leakage, some defective double-paned glass replaced, work done on the elevator, and some woodwork in areas of heavy traffic repainted. In 1985 all the exterior trim was repainted, and the Town set up a reserve fund to save for the eventual replacement of the roof. Both furnishings and carpeting were holding up better than one would expect, given their heavy use, and the Board felt well justified in having paid for top quality when furnishing the building.

Plans for celebrating the tenth anniversary had brewed for several months, led by Trustee president Kathryn Manchester. The month preceding that December date was planned to be full of excitement for all ages; when the time came it lived up to all expectations. A special anniversary issue of *Howe Now* informed the community about the month's events.

Throughout the month an exhibit, "Eighty-Five Years of Howe History," hung in the Mayer Room, featuring historic old photographs, documents, and newspaper clippings tracing the Library's evolution. The exhibit opened with an elegant tea, served as it might have been in Emily Howe's day, complete with flower arrangements and silver service. Residents who, like the Library, were in their eighties, were especially invited and offered transportation, then given flowers upon their arrival.

Trustee and Ray School art teacher Willy Black designed a logo for use on posters and large buttons and oversaw the production of

Logo for ten-year celebration. Created by Willy Black using Diane Haas' 1976 design

immense quantities of the buttons to be distributed at the Library all month.

For the younger children there was, of course, a birthday party, complete with balloons and fun. And since it was a *library* party, author/illustrator Ashley Bryan was invited to read poems and stories. School-age children were guided in groups through the historical exhibit. Katie Manchester related the story of Howe's first 85 years at least 15 times, with personal warmth and with the authority conferred by having used Howe as a child. It soon became clear that, for the students, even the move ten years before was ancient history. A few went home convinced that Katie was a descendent of Emily Howe.

For adults there were special programs each Thursday that month. One of these featured Hanover's Pulitzer prize-winning poet, Richard Eberhart, who read from his work and talked about the background of many of the poems.

Howe librarians hosted a special forum on library automation for public and school librarians in this region. John Kemeny gave the keynote address, "The Fully Automated Reference Library." Dartmouth's president emeritus, himself a pioneer in computing, had in 1961 written a book of prescient essays in which he detailed the ways libraries of the future would be changed by automation. Having read and admired his book while earning her library degree, with no thought that she would ever move to Hanover and meet the author, Patti Eckels took great pleasure in introducing John Kemeny to her colleagues. The State Librarians of both New Hampshire and Vermont were also on hand to report on the emerging automation in their state library systems.

It was clear that Howe would reach the one-million-and-a-half circulation point at some time during this month. A Dartmouth Bookstore gift certificate was to be given to the lucky borrower of that 1,500,000th book, which added tantalizing spice to each library patron's visit and much feverish calculating by the staff in the days leading up to Brenda Schwab's claiming the prize. Unfortunately no one thought to record the title of that 1,500,000th item.

Grand finale to the anniversary month was another birthday party, this one for the grown-ups. Having decided that this should be a celebration, not a fund-raiser, the Corporation subsidized all costs above a moderate charge for the dinner. After wine and hors d'oeuvres in the Mayer Room, 150 guests were served a gourmet dinner at tables appointed with candles, balloons and flowers, set up throughout the main floor of the Library, while Hanover High School string musicians played softly from the loft.

Guests came dressed for a gala evening, and a gala evening it was. John Kemeny, who had spoken at the ground-breaking ceremony eleven years earlier, concluded the occasion with warm personal comments on libraries in general and the Howe Library in particular. Among the attendees, of course, were a great many who had played a role in the realization of this new home for the Library, from serving on committees to raising money to helping move books to their new shelves. As President Kemeny made clear, Howe Library was a symbol of what can be accomplished when caring people work together for the good of their community.

Staffing as the second decade begins

At the 1986 Corporation meeting the Director's[5] report included a section bringing members up to date on the Library staff and the duties of the various members. The responsibilities of most of the staff have been at least partially described earlier in these

5. At about this time the Town changed the title of Howe's head from Librarian to Director, which is used beginning in this chapter.

PHOTO BY HATHORN/OLSON

Library staff in 1985. On stairs: Mary Churchill, Peggy Hyde, Pegge Strickler, Charlotte Bernini. Below: Polly Gould, Mary Soderberg, Jean Watson, Anne Schofield, Ellen Lynch, Patti Eckels (seated), Lurlene Cole, Marcia Manzo.

pages, but there were three newer members about whom less has been said: circulation assistants Marcia Manzo, Charlotte Bernini, and Ann Schofield.

Marcia now had the task of scheduling all staff hours at the circulation and reference desks—a demanding challenge, with 73 hours a week to cover, involving not only regular staff but volunteer and student help as well. Charlotte, who seemed a born teacher, did all the training of new circulation volunteers and students. She also handled the Pick-a-Paperback program, an outreach project begun while still in the old building. Ann, the newest member, had taken on the responsibility for weeding from and adding to some of the special categories of music on records and tapes.

Peggy Hyde, in addition to her former duties, was by now in full charge of both the annual book discussion series and the Elden Murray Photography Contest and Exhibit, and she had designed the extensive historical exhibit featured during the anniversary celebration.

"As we move into our second decade in this building," the Director's report concluded, "we are blessed with a truly superb staff. They have different backgrounds, temperaments, and talents. But they all share a commitment to library service, pride in the work of the group as a whole, and a desire to keep growing and learning."

Later that year Ellen Lynch, needing more time with her young children, regretfully resigned. Mary Hardy, a professional librarian newly arrived in the Upper Valley, took her place

In 1986 Howe acquired a new microfilm reader-printer to replace the outdated reader. Five years of the *New York Times* with indexes were now available on microfilm, in addition to the *Valley News* and the *Hanover Gazette*. Another valuable acquisition was the Hanover Historical Society's gift of a public address system for the Mayer Room.

After conducting a survey of Library patrons, the staff made plans to begin adding videotapes to the circulating collection when funds became available. These were to be informational in nature (travel, science, and art, for example) with a few classic films. Staff and patrons alike felt that popular entertainment films were readily available elsewhere and would not be the best use of the Library's resources.

More planning already?

In the spring the Town Manager urged Board and staff to begin work on a long-range plan for the Library's future, as he had earlier suggested. A committee comprised of the Director and three other staff members, along with Trustee Charles Widmayer, and librarians Andrea Thorpe from the Town Library in Etna and Jean Keene from the Ray School was approved by the Board. They worked through the spring and summer on the plan, projecting facilities, staffing, services, collections, and automation needs over the next five to ten years.

When this committee delivered their 28-page report to the Board in the fall, the initial reaction to the scope of the planning was one of shocked disbelief; the Selectmen's reaction was much the same. This was probably understandable, since everyone felt the Library was still "new," even though facilities and staff were both straining under constantly increasing service pressures. The plan suggested that by the early nineties there should be "serious thought given to planning for expansion." But few were ready to think about this, although the building had been projected—after cost estimates had forced a reduction in square footage—to be adequate for 15 years, and nearly 11 of those years had now passed. The Director, who presented the report, later described the reaction of both groups as "shoot the messenger."

In late 1986 it became apparent that, for various reasons, the 1987-88 budget year would be a most difficult one for the Town. In December the Selectmen's representative on Howe's Board reported political pressure to cut the Library's expenditures. It was alleged, she explained, that the Library budget had risen too much in the past ten years and that libraries (as opposed to police, fire, etc.) are considered "soft services," translated as "non-essential."

This news, of course, came at a bad time, on the heels of the Long Range Plan. One top priority of that plan was the hiring of an assistant director, in order to reduce the Director's work week to a reasonable number of hours, and also to provide continuity when she retired. In addition to other cuts, the Town Manager suggested combining a vacant half-time reference position with a half-time assistant director, to make a start on what both he and the Director considered essential, but the Selectmen felt they could not approve even this.

"Twenty years is a good round number"

On January 1, 1987, the staff gave Patti Eckels a surprise 20th anniversary party, marking the occasion with a gift to Howe's book fund in her honor. They also introduced the first (and only) issue of *The Howe Hoot*, an ingenious tongue-in-cheek publication designed to celebrate the past twenty years and pay tribute to the lighter side of Library life. A favorite item, headlined "Director Rises to New Heights," reported: "While Library staff looked on in envy Patricia Eckels devised a plan to rise quickly in her profession. Mounting the platform of a nearby forklift, she instantly mastered the control mechanism and, wielding a heavy vacuum cleaner, freshened the dusty Bicentennial quilt." True story: the forklift had been parked for lunch break by the workmen changing the highest light

PATRICIA WOOD ECKELS

Twenty years ago, in January of 1967, a new librarian took over the direction of Howe Library. For the Hanover community it was a happening of great good fortune. In the two decades since your arrival, Patti, the Howe Library has enjoyed the finest period in its 86-year history, a period marked by steady growth in all its traditional and new operations and capped by the construction of the building in which we meet today. Permeating all this development has been a very special spirit of competent and friendly service that comes basically from the example you set for the excellent staff assembled around you.

Today you are busy keeping abreast of modern library technology and planning ways to make Howe an even greater asset to the Hanover community in years to come. You have fulfilled a number of important responsibilities for the statewide library system. In 1974 the New Hampshire Library Trustees Association named you Ideal Librarian of the Year, but to members of the Howe Library Corporation you have earned that distinction in every one of your twenty years in Hanover. In this anniversary year, we express to you our heartfelt thanks, our admiration, and, above all, our affectionate regard.

HANOVER, NEW HAMPSHIRE
JANUARY 27, 1987

Citation read by Board President Charles Widmayer at the January 1987 meeting of the corporation.

bulbs and the quilt, previously unreachable, did look much better after its vacuuming. So much for "new heights."

Later that month, acknowledging to the Board and the Town Manager that she felt both unable and unwilling to continue carrying the heavy workload without assistance, Patti made the decision to retire at the end of July. As she reported to the Corporation at their annual meeting, "Twenty years is a good round number...Fresh ideas, energy and leadership will be good for Howe." Shc knew that she was leaving behind a strong, service-oriented staff and, personally, she looked forward to more time with her family and an opportunity to read "real books rather than book reviews."

The Town Manager formed a search committee consisting of himself, Dartmouth's Director of Libraries Margaret Otto, two Trustees and one staff member. The position was nationally advertised, and by spring there were more than one hundred applicants, of whom six would be interviewed.

Still trying to cope with the budget constraints imposed by the Selectmen, the Board reluctantly agreed to their request to raise the non-resident fee to $70 per family in the 1987-88 budget. Hanover-Dresden teachers who did not live in Hanover and non-resident Town employees were also to be charged the fee, and an annual $10 fee was instituted for non-resident Dresden students. Since Howe had historically believed it important to make the Library available on an equal basis to all Hanover-Dresden students and teachers, this was a hard pill to swallow.

The Trustees continued their discussion of the Long Range Plan. By April they were able to reach consensus on implementing those of its recommendations which had no budgetary implications. Gift monies were used to begin the video collection and to provide a TV/VCR in the Mayer Room for Library and community meeting use. Once again James Wicker's thoughtful Librarian's Discretionary Fund had helped Howe to move forward in a new direction. The Board also agreed to encourage more cooperative planning between Howe and the Town library in Etna. For a few years there had been no member of the Town library board interested in sitting on Howe's Board. Now that Fran Baschnagle was filling that position there would again be a liaison between the two.

In June of 1987, Edward Connery Lathem, dean emeritus of the Dartmouth College Libraries, resigned as Trustee, a position he had filled admirably for 20 years. The Board thanked him for his "expertise as a distinguished librarian, his knowledge and love of the world of books, and his wisdom in matters great and small." Edward Lathem was the only Trustee who had served during Patti Eckels' entire twenty-and-one-half-year tenure. Times had changed, and Board members came and went much more frequently than in Howe's earlier years.

PHOTO BY PEGGY HYDE

Trustee Katie Manchester regales the retiree with "Ode to Patti" at the farewell picnic.

At the end of that month, Patti, too, departed, after a public reception given by the Town where old friends and colleagues came to wish her well. She had asked the Board not to give her a formal party, suggesting a picnic instead. To her amazement, they produced a perfect picnic in the Mayer Room one June evening, complete with wading pool, bountiful buffet, and plastic insects. Trustees and staff all sat on beach towels on the floor and laughed over humorous tributes and reminiscences. They then presented Patti with a handsome teak and wrought iron bench for her lakeside camp. It was, she said, her idea of a perfect finale.

TEN

Automating, Updating, Communicating

1987 – 1992

A new Director

ANN TREMENTOZZI was chosen as Howe's new Director. She had begun her library career as head of the public library in Louisville, Colorado, but was anxious to return to her New England roots. That summer, while settling her family in Norwich, she began familiarizing herself with the Library and its staff. At their September meeting, where she met the full Board, the Trustees made plans for a reception to introduce her to the Corporation and the public.

In October 1987 the treasurer reported the welcome news that the Library's investment portfolio had "survived the recent severe drop in the stock market without excessive depreciation." To add to that portfolio, he also announced a large bequest from Evelyn Hansen Hurd, its income designated in part for music-related expenditures. This immediately funded the beginning of the compact disc collection, more frequent tuning for the piano, music programs for children, and the Bach study group at the Library.

Ann Trementozzi, Director of Howe Library 1987–1992

The Trustees, who were preparing some by-law changes for vote at the January 1988 Corporation meeting, incorporated into them a policy on confidentiality of Library circulation records. Howe had always followed such a policy, but because of recent challenges by law enforcement officers in some states, demanding to examine borrowing records of suspected criminals, the Director recommended that Howe should formally declare its intent to protect patron privacy.

Ann Trementozzi's five years as Howe's Director were marked by her plans for automation and for further implementation of the goals of the Long Range Plan. Always hovering in the background, however, and limiting what could be done, were the financial difficulties the Town was encountering in the late eighties and early nineties.

Attempting to fund automation within the growing budget constraints, the Director volunteered in her 1988-89 budget proposal to freeze the book budget for five years in exchange for a small amount of support from the Town toward automating the circulation system. Near the end of that first year she proposed to the Board a system costing $35,000, to be phased in over three years, with the Corporation paying $10,000 annually and the Town being asked for a total of $5,000. The plan was to begin by automating the circulation system, later adding acquisition and cataloging modules, in an attempt "to realize some economies in staff time and provide better public service." With the Board's support, a decision to purchase the Winnebago system was made in April 1989.

The targeted date for bringing the circulation system on-line was originally January 1991. But first, records for 55,000 books and for

FLYING SQUIRREL GRAPHICS

FLYING SQUIRREL GRAPHICS

Volunteers Dick Mayer and Dale Bryant working with Howe's first automated circulation system

the audiovisual collections had to be entered into the database. Computerized records for half the book titles could be purchased commercially; volunteers and work-study students from Dartmouth helped the staff with the daunting task of entering data for the remaining materials and then bar-coding the entire collection.

By October 1991 circulation was finally on-line, its total cost having risen to $50,000. Unfortunately the system, which had been designed for school libraries, was far from perfect for a public library of Howe's size and scope, and (as other libraries had found when automating) it did not require less staff time. But it was a first step toward full automation at Howe.

Between 1989 and 1991 the Library's budget was essentially level-funded by the Town. Then, in the 1991-92 budget, Howe's share of departmental cuts resulted in the Library being open eight fewer hours per week and in a staffing reduction of one full-time equivalent. Since Library use continued to grow, the strain on the staff of trying to provide more service in fewer hours was severe. The book budget, held constant since 1988 as agreed, was now cut even further, so that it was below the dollar level for 1987-88. Howe now had 25% less to spend for collections than would have been needed just to compensate for inflation. Building maintenance had also suffered and this was beginning to show. The Corporation was increasingly called upon to compensate for the cuts where possible.

Updating the Long Range Plan

As for the Long Range Plan, in 1988 the Town Manager asked the Board for an update of priorities in the plan. The Board felt that "space needs were not yet critical," but recommended moving ahead with plans to divert more of the materials budget from print to audiovisuals, though they expressed concern over a recent large increase in non-print circulation, accompanied by a decrease in the circulation of printed materials.

As always, Library usage was reflecting changing life-styles. Borrowers wanted more videos for both adults and children, more books on tape, and more CDs. Libraries everywhere were responding, often reluctantly, since librarians and their boards had traditionally been attuned to the printed word.

Another Board priority was expanding off-site outreach to seniors. Ann Trementozzi began presenting very popular book talks at the Hanover Senior Center and The Greens. And Howe began what was to become an annual senior art exhibit, with work of the area's elder artists on view in the Mayer Room for a month each winter. Volunteer Chrysanthi Bien has ably organized this senior exhibit since its inception.

The Trustees also endorsed as a priority finding new ways to cooperate with other libraries in the region. Howe had long been involved with a public library buying co-op to obtain better discounts on book purchases. It now joined in a new plan, cooperating with other public libraries in the Upper Valley to assemble a collection of videotapes that would rotate among them.

"Worth a million dollars"

The needs of the building itself could not be relegated to the back burner indefinitely. Ventilation in the loft area, long a summer subject of public complaint, had to be addressed. A ventilation expert confirmed what public and staff had long known: the architects' solution of placing huge exhaust fans in the loft ceiling had never been effective. In 1989, at last, the staff's plea to have openable windows at either end of the loft was answered. For good measure, the Corporation installed paddle fans at several locations in the building.

A library built in Hanover at the end of the 20th century would no doubt have been air-conditioned. But in the early seventies, when this building was planned, air conditioning was considered a luxury not needed in northern New England; and the building's open design meant that it was not an option that could easily be added later.

In 1990, to alleviate the very crowded situation in the staff work area, the Corporation funded planning, construction, and furnishings for moving technical services to a new space fashioned from part of the basement. Workspaces in the main floor workroom were then reconfigured. This was a $53,000 project but one that, together with the loft ventilation, prompted one staff member to describe the changes as "worth a million dollars in improved efficiency and morale."

The following year the Corporation redecorated the Murray Room to make it more comfortable and take some of the meeting room traffic out of the Mayer Room.

Corporation and Town define their partnership

During this time the Trustees began working with the Board of Selectmen on a Memo of Understanding, which would "outline their mutual assumptions guiding Town and Corporation financing for the Library." This was an area where there had been misunderstandings at times because there had, of course, been many changes in the membership of both boards since they began working together in the early seventies. Communication between the two groups clearly needed work. Also the Corporation's financial picture had changed. Gifts and bequests to Howe had increased greatly in those 20 years; the mortgage on the Nichols property would be paid off in 1992; and payment on the Corporation's construction loan would be completed by 1995. Some articulated plan for sharing Library financing was needed, as was an annual budget plan for the Corporation, which had previously had little income not committed to debt reduction.

The resulting Statement of Understanding included these words: "The boards expect the Town to continue to fund the operating expenses of the Library at a level consistent with the type and size of a public library appropriate to Hanover... the funds of the Corporation should be used to enhance the library facilities and collections beyond what can be expected from tax revenues. Corporation funds will not be used to fund regular operating expenses such as salaries, supplies, utilities and related costs."

Glimpses of Library life

Some things seemed never to change. The urge to find the right role for a Friends group was one, and in early 1992 the Board agreed to sponsor yet another incarnation of a Friends of the Library program. Unlike previous short-lived attempts, this program would have no organizational structure or officers; it would simply serve as a vehicle to communicate with users and friends about the Library's activities and needs and to encourage their individual volunteer help and financial support.

Another familiar problem to be solved was the everlasting question of how to deal with teen-agers spending their after-school hours at Howe and needing more behavioral supervision that the staff had time to give. The Library again sent a letter to parents of Richmond and Hanover High students asking their cooperation, and a new Code of Behavior for young people was posted.

Soon after, Howe and Dartmouth librarians held a workshop at Howe for 80 Dresden teachers to discuss with them the impact of mass assignments on their libraries and the best ways for the teachers to provide them with advance notice. Though during much

Portrait of Norma W. Fiske, whose bequest in 1991 was the Library's largest gift ever

of the 20th century Hanover schools had been served only by Howe, there were now fine libraries in the schools. But students still needed to supplement them with the breadth and depth of Howe's collection, and Howe's staff was anxious to provide the most effective help possible.

In return, when eighth graders began doing community service as part of their curriculum, several came to Howe to be trained in shelving books, weeding out old magazines, etc. Howe also continued to work with college students. Pegge Strickler had first begun advising Dartmouth students who were studying children's literature in their education classes. Now she supplied books and advice to Tucker Foundation volunteers who were serving as "book buddies" for some Upper Valley children.

In 1991 Norma Fiske, long-time Corporation member and Library friend, died and left her estate of more than $325,000 to Howe. This was—and is still—by far the largest gift ever made to Howe. Later that year the Trustees established a fund to honor their former president, Charles Widmayer, after his death. Howe now had 21 named funds, many restricted to specific uses.

Adult evening programs during the Trementozzi years took a new form. The volunteer book selection advisory and the program planning committees were discontinued and weekly programs presented by volunteers from the community were phased out.

PHOTO BY STEPHANIE WOLFF

The "unflappable" Mary Churchill who retired in 1992 after a record 43 years at Howe

However, there were frequent well-attended book discussion series, led by scholars funded through the New Hampshire Council on the Humanities and with books paid for by the Elden Murray Fund.

As always, there were staff changes in these years. When Jean Watson and Lurlene Cole both retired, Hillary Platt became technical services assistant. The Town funded a new position in 1988, and Janice Blake became the Library's first secretary (later office manager), relieving the Director of many time-consuming responsibilities.

Pegge Strickler and Mary Churchill both retired in the fall of 1992 and were honored at receptions to give the community a chance to express its appreciation. Pegge had given 20 innovative and productive years to nurturing the Library's children's services, and Mary had spent 43 years helping keep Howe afloat through vastly changing times.

Mary was featured in the Library's winter newsletter that year. Her grateful colleagues thanked her for "thinking clearly, being patient beyond all reasonable expectation, laughing with gusto, and whistling Bach." With Pegge and Mary gone, there was no longer anyone on the staff who dated back to the "olden days" in Emily Howe's house.

Joanne Blais joined the Howe staff as children's librarian immediately after Pegge's retirement. Joanne had earned her library degree at the University of Denver and worked in a public library setting with both children and young adults. After moving to Vermont she had for six years been "head librarian, children's specialist, reference librarian, cataloger and janitor," in her words, at the one-woman Wilder Public Library before coming to Howe.

Director Trementozzi resigned in November 1992. Town Manager Vermilya asked Peggy Hyde to become Acting Director for "a few months" and the search began again for a new Director for Howe.

ELEVEN

A Cool Head in Difficult Times

1993 – 1994

PEGGY FORSTER HYDE knew Howe and the local community well, having grown up in Hanover. After college, while serving as a school librarian in Greenwich, Connecticut, she had started working toward a graduate library science degree in the evening. This course of study had been interrupted when her family moved to California, where she worked part-time in a public library system.

After coming back to Hanover she had put her library experience to good use at Howe, first as a volunteer in 1976, then as a paid substitute, and finally as a regular staff member. Well organized, articulate, always warm and generous, Peggy had the respect and affection of all the staff and volunteers. She was the ideal person to lead the Library through this stressful period, which lengthened to 18 months before a permanent Director was finally in place.

"How to do more with less"

That Peggy thoroughly understood Howe's current situation was evident in her orientation session for new Trustees and Corporation members in early 1993. The challenge of the nineties would be, she predicted, "how to do more with less." Evaluating Howe's programs in light of the current economic climate, she asked, "What are our primary roles? What services will grow, which face extinction? To what aspects of Library activity is the Corporation financially committed beyond what the Town can do? Collection development? Automation? Building expansion?"

She pointed out that Howe was badly understaffed, never having recovered from the staffing cut in the 1991-92 year. And, because the physical crowding had become acute, it was imperative for the Board to begin planning for long-term space needs. In general, the Acting Director took a pro-active role in better acquainting the Trustees with the personnel, organization, and functioning of the Library. In these efforts she was helped greatly by the Board's new president, David Goudy, whose experience in directing the Montshire Museum and working with its Trustees was invaluable. Together they saw to it that the full Board now had regular, concise, easily understood reports with which to achieve a better understanding of their current challenges.

Board activism

David Goudy encouraged taking a new look at the way in which the Board functioned, focusing on setting new goals, discovering what abilities were needed to reach these goals, and then selecting Trustees who possessed specific abilities. Matt Marshall, with his skills in community relations and access to the business community, and Steve Marion, with his expertise in planning at the medical center, were brought on the Board at this time. Dale Bryant, with her incisive thinking and her volunteer's understanding of the staff's needs and perspectives was a similarly targeted choice for Trustee.

David Goudy also saw urgency in expanding the Statement of Understanding with the Selectmen and in establishing an investment committee to review the Corporation's investments and make recommendations for long-term financial management of the portfolio. This review was completed in 1994.

Based on a consultant's recommendations and their own modifications, the staff proposed in early 1993 a significant reallocation of the public space in the main part of the Library. Their plan would create better browsing areas for the dramatically growing audiovisual collections, provide adequate and more inviting space for the young adult area, and create places for public access computers and more reference technology.

Intended to meet space needs on the main floor for three more years, the plan was approved by the Board and funded by the Corporation. Later that year a new roof for the building was completed, with more insulation added for energy conservation. Fortunately the Town had been budgeting capital reserve funds for the roof over several years.

On the real estate front in 1993, the Nichols property lease to tenants expired and was renewed for 18 months. The Walpole Woodlot saga had continued to resurface from time to time, with no action taken. The Board now voted to put the lot in "current use" to reduce property taxes, which had increased to $1,900 annually. Although the lot had been reassessed from $20,000 to $92,000, no realtor was interested in listing it because of a declining real estate market.

A particularly happy event for the Library and the community that year was the auction of Josephine Wolfenden's art for the benefit of Howe. Jo, who had died the year before, was a long-time and very active resident of Hanover and a painter of considerable skill. Howe had exhibited her work in 1987 and she had bequeathed to

Howe for auction the paintings remaining in her collection. Family and friends came from near and far for the reception/auction, which was a memorable community gathering.

Winnebago System re-evaluated

By June of 1993 it was evident that the Winnebago automation system was not sophisticated enough for Howe's needs and would need to be replaced before the Library could add an automated catalog. The staff began to plan for a more effective system.

The technical services department had been in limbo since Mary Churchill's departure in late 1992. Polly Gould had taken over temporarily, aided by part time help from other staff. But by this time technical services involved not only ordering, receiving, cataloging and processing new materials, but also being the systems management coordinator for automation. It became obvious that Howe could no longer wait for a permanent director to arrive before finding new leadership for this department.

In November 1993 Victoria Bedi, an experienced technical services librarian, joined the staff. The first technical services director at Howe to have prior experience with automated systems, she immediately took the leadership in searching for the system that could best meet the Library's specific needs. Once she had found the system she would recommend, she would be responsible for educating the staff, Board, and Selectmen and convincing them of its merits.

With the support of the Town Manager, Peggy Hyde proposed, in her 1993-94 budget request, to return to the circulation staffing levels existing before the reductions three years earlier. The strain on staff was increasingly serious, especially with a major portion of Peggy's time being given to her role as Acting Director. These staff hours were gradually restored during Peggy's tenure.

She also worked successfully to convince the Town that part-time substitutes who had regular duties but had never been given "permanent" status should now be classified as such and be able to accrue sick leave and vacation time on a prorated basis. The three women affected at that time by this change in status were Cindy Varnum, Joan Ridgeway, and Natalie Urmson. Each had been a steady source of support, staffing the circulation desk during vacations and illnesses and assuming additional duties for which other staff had no time.

In that budget year the staff was overjoyed when the Selectmen also approved resuming the custom of issuing free cards for nonresident teachers in the Hanover and Dresden schools. Soon after, the schools and Town agreed on an arrangement whereby the Town

FLYING SQUIRREL GRAPHICS

After a reader of the Library newsletter suggested possible gender imbalance, some staffers posed for this photo for the next issue. Left to right: "Andrew" Schofield, "Charlie" Bernini, "Patrick" Hyde, "Allen" Lynch, "Victor" Bedi, "Nathaniel" Urmson, "Jan" Grady.

would resume providing free cards to all Dresden students (including Norwich) and the schools would pay a small fee for each tuitioned student.

The search re-opened

The expectation of all concerned had been that a new Director would be in place in mid-1993. By March there were 47 candidates for the position, of whom the search committee unanimously recommended one. When he decided not to re-locate, the search had to begin anew. Knowing her tenure would be continuing longer than originally expected, Peggy Hyde developed a new organizational pattern to support her administrative duties, creating a management team consisting of public services librarian Polly Gould, circulation supervisor Mary Soderberg, and Vicki Bedi of technical services. The Town Manager approved this team approach on a trial basis and was sufficiently impressed that he later borrowed it to use as a model for the Town's own team management.

A renewed search for Library Director produced 83 applicants, the two strongest coming from California for interviews over the summer. The successful candidate planned to make the move East by the year's end, but bad luck continued to plague the search process. After several delays for personal crises (including earthquake damage to her home) she finally withdrew from the position. Mr. Vermilya then reviewed previous applications and without further delay appointed Marlene McGonigle as Director, to begin May 15, 1994. She was well qualified for the position, with broad professional experience, having directed the public library in Kinelton, New Jersey, where the population, staff size, and budget were similar to Howe's. Prior to that she had been a school librarian for several years.

Marlene McGonigle, appointed Director of Howe Library in May 1994

In June, shortly after Marlene's arrival, the Town closed the Library for two days so that the new Director and her staff could spend that time in a retreat, getting acquainted and setting priorities for both the immediate future and the longer term. This retreat, which provided an optimal transition, was essentially a morale building thank-you gift from the Town to the Howe staff for their extended months of extraordinary effort in absorbing the usual work of a Director while continuing to serve the public with never-failing good cheer.

During those 18 months Peggy Hyde, the embodiment of grace under pressure, successfully juggled her many added responsibilities; worked effectively with the Trustees, the Town management, and the public; and kept staff morale high. Now she gratefully relinquished the hat of Acting Director and provided strong support as Marlene McGonigle was introduced to the "culture" of the Howe Library and expertly took over its leadership.

TWELVE

The Library in the Computer Age

1994 – 1999

The technology explosion

ON THROUGH the decade, technology and its impact on library services continued to be a major theme. No matter where one's opinion fell in the range of enthusiasm for computers, everyone responsible for library planning realized that there could be no return to the old days and that the emphasis needed to be on making wise choices in this rapidly changing new library world.

In September of 1994 Vicki Bedi's task force, after researching integrated library systems in use at other public libraries and making site visits to 11 of these, recommended purchasing Innopac, the same system used by Dartmouth libraries. Director Marlene McGonigle found that her first administrative challenge at Howe was overseeing the full implementation of this system. Acquiring Innopac required a major financial commitment, for which she secured the unanimous approval of the Board of Selectmen and the Howe Trustees. The Corporation agreed to contribute $150,000 and the Town $100,000. A year later the new circulation system and Howe's first automated public access catalog were up and running.

The user-friendly catalog was christened "KnowHowe" after a contest to name it, with second place going to "Aunty Em." (The latter was not as descriptive, but it did have a reassuringly nostalgic ring for patrons who felt technologically challenged.) In addition to catalog and circulation functions, Innopac also provided acquisition, serials, and management report modules.

With volunteer trainers on hand to help neophytes, patrons quickly came to appreciate KnowHowe, and those with their own PC's appreciated the ability they soon had to access their borrowing records and the catalog from home or office. Users of KnowHowe also had access through it to the Dartmouth College

FLYING SQUIRREL GRAPHICS

Ellen Hollaender instructs fellow volunteer Dorothy Heeremans in the use of Know-Howe, 1995.

catalog. Howe Library now had an automated system fully capable of meeting its present needs and those of the foreseeable future.

Innopac's more sophisticated circulation system required intensive initial training and an ongoing time commitment of at least six hours weekly. Marj Boley was the only one of the full complement of circulation desk volunteers who faithfully continued in that role for the next several years, while she also served ably as a Trustee. A second circulation volunteer, Christine Eickelman, joined her in 1997.

However, volunteers could and did help with other facets of the automated system, including such projects as transferring Howe's community organization file to an easily updated electronic format. Total volunteer hours, which had been in decline since 1987, began to increase, especially in technical services.

By early 1996 public access to the internet was available at Howe, jointly financed by the Corporation and a federal grant through the State Library. Reference staff became well-versed in answering queries via multiple databases. Volunteers helped new internet users on a one-to-one basis. More formal group training sessions were also offered, with an enthusiastic attendance of 80 at the first of these. This was quite a leap from 1985 when Howe had acquired its first PC and made it, with software and manuals, available for self-teaching. The Library and ValleyNet, a non-profit internet provider Howe had helped to develop, have continued to jointly sponsor programs on various aspects of the internet, with some of these sessions taped for the local cable channel.

Questions of intellectual freedom

Public internet access at Howe naturally prompted the Trustees to discuss the Library's intellectual freedom policies as applied to the internet. A new national group calling itself Family Friendly

Libraries had proclaimed the American Library Association and its Library Bill of Rights to be "hostile to traditional family values" in making uncensored use of the internet available to all. After studying this issue the Board reaffirmed its support for the Library Bill of Rights by stating,

> *"the Library cannot control or monitor information on the internet, nor can it be held responsible for any material accessed through it. Parents or other legal guardians are responsible for their children's use of the internet, just as they are for their use of materials in the library's collection."*

However, Howe does urge parents to supervise children's use of the internet in general and calls attention to the lack of regulation or standards for material found there.[6]

The year 1997 saw considerable technological innovation locally. Etna Library's holdings came on-line, a new Libraries of Hanover card made its debut, and volunteers provided courier service between the two libraries. The expectation was that in the future the school libraries' catalogs would be joined to the Howe-Etna data base and the card would be honored at all those libraries. At this writing the schools' data base is still not compatible with Howe's, but the hope continues that all Hanover's libraries will one day be available via one catalog and one card.

Howe's staff had in 1994 developed websites for both the Town and Howe, both of which it continues to maintain. Then, in 1997, Howe and ValleyNet worked together to create an on-line community calendar of events, using software Dartmouth had developed for its own calendar. Any non-profit organization was immediately eligible to join by adding its own events or forwarding

6. The debate on this issue of "protecting" minors from the internet, or "censoring" intellectual freedom, depending on one's viewpoint, continues with no end in sight. At this writing the ALA, the ACLU and other first-amendment rights advocates are still embroiled in court battles over laws requiring librarians to screen internet use.

FLYING SQUIRREL GRAPHICS

Ten-year award recipients, from left to right: Jeanne Baumgartner, Kathy Stickney, Marian DeLill, Priscilla Weismann, Lari Widmayer, Elaine Harp, Pam Doenges, Louise Bowen, Kit Farrell, Patty Radway, Anne Mellor, Dorothy Talbot, John Snell. Absent: Chrysanthi Bien, Dorothy Heeremans.

them to ValleyNet for entry. Howe and ValleyNet have continued to maintain the ValleyNet's bank of communications equipment.

That same year, Howe subscribed to an on-line database of periodicals, which provided full-text access and indexing for 394 magazines, including backfiles to 1984. By 1998 this had grown to over 1,000 periodicals, and two years later grew to more than 2,800 titles when the State Library subscribed to ProQuest database for all libraries in the New Hampshire State Network. This not only provided a valuable service for Library patrons but also relieved Howe of the need to store backfiles of these periodicals, thereby releasing staff from running up and down stairs to retrieve back issues—a significant time-saver when school research assignments were heavy.

Marlene McGonigle was appointed to the New Hampshire Technology Task Force. This was now where the action was in state aid for public libraries. The old statewide system with Service Center libraries and accreditation of libraries at various levels, with aid based on these levels, which Patti Eckels had helped develop and promote 20 years before, was now outmoded. Since the legislature had never funded it to any significant degree, there had been little incentive for libraries to comply with standards. Now, with changing ways of sharing information, the State Library's emphasis was on encouraging libraries to make use of the technological resources available. It served as the center of the newly automated union catalog and offered support through continuing education in the various phases of automation.

"If Andrew and Emily were here today"

The State Library Network began requiring a Board-approved Technology Plan from its member libraries in 1998.

Howe's staff produced a thoughtful, comprehensive Technology Plan for the Trustees' approval at their April 1998 meeting. The plan was based on Howe's Mission Statement and Long Range Plan, and the staff's presentation to the Board was prefaced by a one-page overview of the changing modes of providing information during 20th century library history. Posing the attention-getting question, "Would Andrew Carnegie and Emily Howe be rolling in their graves?" the staff concluded:

> *"If Andrew and Emily were here today . . . would they found a small public library whose services were limited to a collection of books and a few standard print reference sources? Would they place a value judgment on the various forms in which knowledge is delivered? Or would they nod approvingly at the Howe Library mission to 'bring together people, ideas and information' as consistent with [their own early mission to provide free access to books]? Would they understand that fulfilling this mission in the 21st century would involve heavy reliance on technology?... Would they not, in their wisdom, appreciate that achieving Howe Library's service goals as set forth in the Technology Plan would enhance the accessibility and value of our most treasured resource: the book? Technology may have changed the way we do things, but not what we aim to do. Surely Andrew and Emily would understand."*

This statement sparked a useful philosophical discussion on the changing emphasis in allocation of the Library's financial resources. There were certainly Trustees with reservations about these changes. But the meeting ended in a unanimous vote to approve the Plan, specifying only that it should be clear Howe did not aim to be "on the cutting edge" in technology but to "make the best use of proven technological resources, within the constraints of the budget."

In March of 1999 Howe took the final major step in its 20th century automation journey when it installed WebPac, the Innopac module designed to connect the KnowHowe catalog to the internet, thereby enabling Web-based catalog searches. Using the Web, the range of possible search terms is vastly enlarged, and eventually hot links will allow a searcher to jump directly from a record in Howe's catalog to other sites on the Web that house related information.

With Y2K anxiety permeating business and government planning in the latter part of 1999, the Town asked department heads to prepare a list of "mission critical" functions and a contingency plan for each function. Then, on the last evening of the century, Hanover's department heads spent New Year's Eve together at the fire station, sipping sparkling apple juice and waiting until midnight to test computer systems. Fortunately, in Hanover as elsewhere, preparations had been thorough, the systems moved smoothly from 1999 to 2000, and Y2K computer fears proved no more realistic than the millenarian convictions of some religious zealots that Judgment Day was at hand.

Growing pains again

The Long Range Plan referred to above in discussing the Technology Report was the new updated plan, which had been completed in October 1996. By then most of the recommendations from the 1986 plan had been achieved, except for those concerning enlarged facilities.

The 1996 planning committee consisted of Board president Ann Crow as chair; fellow Trustees Fran Baschnagel and Matt Marshall; community representatives Cheryl Boghosian and

Debby Cromwell; and staff members Ellen Lynch and Marlene McGonigle. After seeking input from community focus groups and questionnaires and from various library specialists, they helped the Board to develop a Mission Statement and to identify roles to be emphasized in fulfilling that mission. Then they outlined the main strategies to be pursued. The most significant of these strategies was "Developing a Master Plan to examine the costs and benefits of remodeling the present facility, building an addition for future growth, and providing adequate parking."

Promptly after receiving the committee's report, the Board appointed a master facility planning committee, chaired by Trustee Steve Marion, to work with consultants and review facilities options of various sizes. This committee concluded that only two of the options studied were capable of meeting Library needs for a reasonable period of time: either a major remodeling/addition expanding Howe's area by approximately two-thirds, or a new building on a new downtown site, if one could be found.

As Trustees explained the Library's space needs and discussed their ideas informally with the Selectmen in 1998, it became clear that Town officials felt Howe needed to coordinate the timing of its expansion with the other projects under discussion in the community. Howe was thus given a non-voting seat on the joint public facilities study committee being formed and funded by the Hanover and Norwich Selectboards, Dartmouth College, and the Hanover, Norwich and Dresden school districts.

Retaining a consultant, this committee met regularly over the next few years to work on joint planning for its various constituencies. At that time, new schools, a Hanover Community Center, and Howe's expansion were all in various stages of planning. At times it appeared that if the Middle School were relocated there might be space available to Howe on present school grounds. Or, after

Dartmouth's purchase of several properties in Howe's neighborhood, there might be a new site there for Howe.

In April of 1999, assuming the expansion probably would have to take place on site, Howe's Trustees chose the architectural firm of Robert A.M. Stern to develop a concept and schematic drawings. Stern's plans were presented to the Corporation at their November 1999 annual meeting. But because of continuing site uncertainties the plans were put on hold, although the Board had hoped to announce a definite course of action by the time of Howe's centennial the following spring.

Crowded shelves, growing programs

Meanwhile, in the second half of the 1990s, through all this prolonged planning activity with its studies, reports, consultants, and committees, Howe's staff continued to give the best service it could, rearranging equipment and furnishings to make maximum space for the collections. All seven tiers of shelving were now crowded and no further expansion of the book collection would be possible by the end of the decade. The situation was reminiscent of the early 1970s, when the Library had had to discard one book for each new book added.

There were some changes in collections and programs, however. History repeated itself when a small new donor-financed rental collection of best-sellers began to circulate (supplementing the Library's freely circulating copies) for those who just couldn't wait to read John Grisham's newest. Howe had earlier maintained a rental collection of mysteries, but it had been phased out years before.

The supply of the increasingly popular unabridged books-on-tape grew in 1997, when Upper Valley public libraries developed a cooperative rotating collection of these similar to the rotating group of videos begun earlier. CDRoms, which had first become available for in-house use in 1995, were joined in 1997 by small circulating collections for both adults and children.

In 1997 Kate Tuckerman bequeathed nearly $252,000 to Howe. Kate's late husband, Gustavus Tuckerman, had been an early enthusiast when Howe provided in-house stereo players in the new building, and had often made knowledgeable recommendations on records the Library might add. Kate's will asked that part of the bequest be used in the future to strengthen Howe's collection of musical recordings.

Programming for adults was again alive and well. Book discussion programs with a lecture/discussion format, led by knowledgeable scholars (frequently local scholars Susanne Brown or Laurence Davies) were designed for a wide range of tastes. Topics included *Jane Austen and Her Times, Fiction and the Historical*

FLYING SQUIRREL GRAPHICS

Teen-aged pages at Howe, 1996. Left to right: Ian Struckoff, Amelia Talbert, Brian Searle, Danielle DuBois, Dan Warbel-Sanborn

Moment, *The American Wilderness*, and *Contemporary American Poetry After Robert Frost*. One participant likened these series to "a ride in an open carriage through the land of ideas."

High school student and Howe page Ian Struckhoff developed a new month-long exhibit at Howe in 1994 and 1995 to feature computer-generated art. It was called *Canvas of the Future* and especially attracted the attention of the young adults.

From October 1998 through May 1999 a series of programs on *Visions of the Millennium* drew large audiences. Scholars from the fields of literature, art, history, computer science, religion, and astronomy gave talks about Millenarian views, fears, and beliefs from Biblical times to our own.

In the fall of 1999 Howe began to co-sponsor, with independent film historian and curator Bruce Posner, a *Lovers of Cinema* series, presenting rare independent and artist-made films and videos as well as lost classics from the early days of cinema. Posner's series went on to the Whitney Museum and then to Moscow and will be traveling to Chicago, Berlin, Los Angeles, Paris, and beyond through 2005. Howe was its premier location.

The Elden Murray Photo Contest was, in the spring of 2000, in its twenty-fourth year of showcasing local photographic talent. That year, for the first time, the Upper Valley Camera Club took over the administrative work of this exhibit from the Library staff.

Innovations in the children's department

Interest in service to children also continued to grow. Children's librarian Joanne Blais added a story time for two's and three's to the preschool story schedule in 1995, and the following year she created an innovative Toddler Time playgroup for the very youngest children and their caregivers. This informal weekly program was

FLYING SQUIRREL GRAPHICS

Joanne Blais reading to preschoolers, 1994: Zachary, Alex and Megan appear captivated.

FLYING SQUIRREL GRAPHICS

an immediate hit and became a vehicle for both adults and children to get to know the Library and make new friends. There were picture books, toys, and snacks for the children, while their mothers (who might be new to the area or to parenting) could meet and talk. By the year 2000, the average attendance at this program was 15 to 20 children, with their caregivers.

Special programs continued on Saturdays and during vacations. Some of the most successful of these were an Audubon Society program on birds (with a live red-tail hawk and a barred owl), Martha Davis with her out-sized puppets, and two visiting folklorists bringing *Tales of the Coyote* from the Southwest.

The summer reading programs grew in popularity, with themes such as *Take Us to Your Readers*, a science fiction/astronomy series. At decade's end about 150 children were involved each summer, contracting to do independent reading and participating in on-site programs and excursions farther afield, such as a trip to the college observatory for the astronomy series.

The phenomenon of home-schooling continued to grow through the nineties. The children's librarian reported working closely with these parents and children to help provide the resources they needed, noting, "they are a very savvy group who certainly know their way around libraries."

In 1996 the Town agreed to make the position of children's librarian full time; it had been filled approximately 30 hours per week since 1971. When Joanne Blais resigned in mid-1998, Denise Reitsma succeeded her. Denise had worked in children's services in the public libraries of Enfield, Canaan and Lebanon and brought her own innovations to the children's department.

After Denise's arrival the children's chess program grew to become a chess club for all ages. And, with gift funds, Howe subscribed to the new One Thousand Books program, wherein 100 sturdy canvas bags, each containing ten carefully selected picture books, were available for checkout to preschoolers. With many mothers now juggling family and career, it was an appreciated time-saver to have recommended and varied books all chosen and "ready to go."

In 1999 the Harry Potter boom was sweeping the country with children of all ages, their parents, and their grandparents avidly following Harry's adventures as wizard-in-training. Denise alluded to this publishing phenomenon in her annual report, telling the Corporation that "Howe has 11 copies and they are never on the shelf."

Dartmouth's children's literature class and Howe's children's department continued their cooperation. The class now had 100 students using Howe's resources, and Howe staff were invited to attend their class lectures by special guest speakers. In a new vein, WDCR in early 2000 began broadcasting the class's Friday afternoon children's program, "Mystery and Myth," before a live (and delighted) audience at Howe. The students dramatized and performed fairytales, and the mostly school-age audience in Howe's Mayer Room found this media experience fascinating.

Organizing the archives

Volunteers continued to work generously to support the staff and to take on projects for which no staff member had time. By decade's end volunteer participation had again attained the level of the mid-eighties. In 1999, reports show 64 volunteers attending the annual luncheon in their honor, which had throughout the nineties been catered by volunteer super chefs Joan Ridgeway and Natalie Urmson. The Hanover Inn graciously loaned china, silverware, and tables for these affairs.

Researching Howe's early years for a talk to the Historical Society in 1996,[7] former director Patti Eckels was reminded that there were archival records scattered all over the basement storage area—in boxes, on shelves, and housed (in no particular order) in the ancient locked metal cabinet always called "the safe." Those records included the original handwritten minutes and ledgers back to 1900, nearly 100 years of financial and statistical data, fragile news-

7. For distribution at this meeting Patti Eckels and Peggy Hyde prepared a two-page timetable showing "Howe Library Trends and Events 1900-1995," which was updated in 2000. This is a helpful distillation of Howe's history until then.

paper clippings, treasured old photographs, and more. Struck by the fact that all this Library history needed to be organized, preserved, and made accessible for the future, she volunteered to begin the task.

It was a daunting job, made far easier by Joan Snell's offer to help. Together they sorted, arranged materials by category in acid-free containers, and inventoried the resulting collection. Later, at staff member Kris Burnett's suggestion, the records would be placed in Rauner Special Collections at Dartmouth for safe preservation; the Corporation provided funding for Rauner to organize and catalog the records, which will be available for future research.

Joan and Patti also inventoried the odd assortment of non-library materials bequeathed to Howe over the years, including the Hitchcock family's autograph collection, a box of valentines from the 1880s, a 15th century wood and polychrome madonna, and records of various long-defunct Hanover groups such as the Fortnightly Club. They made various recommendations to the Board about the possible disposition of these items. The madonna, to everyone's delight, brought $10,000 at auction.

Becoming intrigued with the MBMcC reader's notes in the fronts of some of the old books in the storeroom, Joan then took on the job of locating all the books in the collection with notes by Margaret McCallum, Elaine Harp and others. The staff continued her project by producing attractive booklets about both Margaret and Elaine, with some biographical information and a list of titles annotated by them.

In 1997 Dick Ridgeway, who had helped Howe in many other volunteer capacities, became volunteer curator of Howe's monthly art exhibits, recruiting fellow artists and working with them to organize and hang the exhibits, freeing Howe staff from this responsibility.

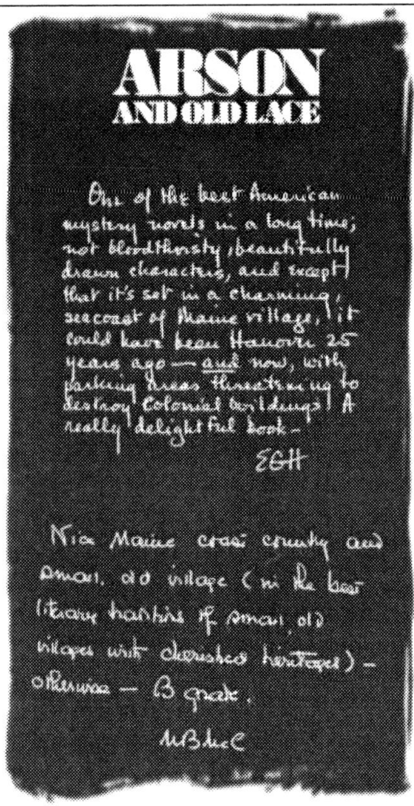

Join the McC Brigade

Ever wonder who is MBMcC, author of the telling little reviews inside so many of Howe's older books? Margaret McCallum, a graduate student at Columbia, moved to Hanover as a bride in the '20s and made extraordinary contributions to Howe Library over many years thereafter. She will be featured in the next issue of *Here's Howe*.

A few of us are now on a treasure hunt, tracking down as many of her comments—and those by other reviewers—as we can find, with the goal of compiling and preserving them for posterity. (Plus, opening each book is a great way to discover off the beaten track good reads.)

All levels of hunters are welcome: tall for the top shelves, agile for the bottom, as well as most for the middle. I am in the library Monday mornings, 10-12 and my phone number is 643-3347. Once you know how we are proceeding, you can continue at your own convenience.

Volunteers Ruth Britton and Joan Snell hunt for readers' notes by MBMcC, EGH, and others.

Board challenges

Among the many invited to the annual volunteer luncheons were the Trustees who, indeed, gave freely of their time working on the Board and its committees. Those generous people who served in this capacity over the course of Howe's century of service are listed with appreciation in Appendix B.

In 1995 the Corporation paid tribute to two Trustees who were retiring after long service, Ruth Young and Leonard Morrissey, Jr. Ruth had served two series of terms on the Board, totaling 22 years and including time as both president and secretary. In addition, she

Leonard Morrissey Jr., Treasurer of the Corporation from 1977 to 1995

had served on the building committee, helped choose furnishings for the new building, and provided refreshments for more meetings and celebrations than could be counted.

Len had, with no experience in the Corporation's finances, become treasurer and taken over the reins, or rather, the numerous boxes of scattered documents, after Maurice Aldrich's untimely death in 1977. With a good humor that belied the complexity of the task, he had deciphered Mr. Aldrich's system, nurtured the investments, and kept impressive financial records. At the end of his tenure the debt on both the Nichols property and the new Library building had been retired, the Corporation's financial year had been synchronized with the Town's fiscal calendar, and the portfolio's value had reached just over $2,000,000.

At the 1995 Corporation meeting, now held in the fall because of the changed fiscal year, Willy Black delivered a tribute to "King Leonard" and "Queen Ruth" in the guise of a fairy tale. Willy herself had at that time served faithfully for 14 years as the Selectmen's representative to the Board.

With Len's retirement, Jean Whitall took over as treasurer. Concerned about its fiduciary responsibility in an increasingly complex financial environment the Board asked its finance committee, chaired by the treasurer, to review the portfolio. On that group's recommendation they then sold all the individual stocks in 1998, reinvesting the proceeds in mutual funds. Two years later the Board chose a local professional firm to help them develop an investment policy and to manage the Corporation's investments. Jean Whitall compiled a notebook thoroughly detailing the history of each named endowed fund. Whereas there had been just four until the mid-1960s, there were 37 by the year 2000. [See Appendix E.]

As planning for a new facility progressed, another focus was the Board's commitment to continually improving communication with the Selectmen. Cliff Vermilya, who had already done much to improve this communication, retired in 1996 after outstanding service to Hanover. The new Town Manager, Julia Griffin, was invited to meet informally with the staff and to attend a Board meeting soon after her arrival. From the beginning she extended herself to become informed about the activities and needs of the Library.

In October of 1998 the Trustees wrote to the Selectmen suggesting an update of their 1992 Statement of Understanding, declaring their own willingness to consider raising a building expansion fund that would include "an endowment which could help support some programs and professional staff . . . to modify the impact [of expansion] on the operating increases requested from the Town."

They hoped for a discussion of what increased level of support the Town would be able to undertake. But Hanover was about to feel the impact of the new statewide property tax to equalize school funding in New Hampshire, and the Selectmen hesitated to make any commitment until that impact could be assessed.

As it regularly had done, the Board used Corporation income to fund various improvements to the Library and its furnishings. In the late 1990s these included new carpeting in traffic areas on the main floor, reupholstery of all the large chairs in the Mayer Room and some of the seating on the main floor, improved lighting in the periodical room, and additional paddle fans for ventilation. Corporation funds also purchased a locked cabinet for display of jazz and pop CDs (so that they no longer must be shelved behind the desk for safekeeping), and a new reference desk with a recessed area for the computer, which now played a major role in reference librarians' work.

Finally, the last chapter was written in one very old piece of Corporation business: the Walpole Woodlot Saga came to an end when the property was logged in 1996 and then sold in 1998 for $45,000.

Staff Who's Who at century's end

When Marlene McGonigle became Howe's director in 1994 her administrative skills had immediately been apparent. She saw at once the critical importance of a good working relationship between the Howe Board and the Hanover Selectmen and Town Manager, and considered the role of liaison between these two groups one of her top priorities.

Administrative skills were equally apparent in her leadership of the staff as she presided over that first productive staff retreat, demonstrating her ability to build consensus within the team management model. As one staff member recalls, "Marlene effectively organized us to initiate planning and changes so that change really came from the staff. We each felt ownership and enthusiasm for implementing new ideas."

During her tenure there were, as always, changes in the makeup and responsibilities of Library staff, in addition to those already mentioned in the children's room

In 1996 reference librarian Ellen Lynch, who had returned to Howe in 1993, became coordinator of public services, replacing Polly Gould. Polly had chosen to reduce her hours but continued to work in both public services and technical services. Kristina Burnett, former librarian at Cardigan Mountain School, joined the staff as part-time circulation assistant.

The Town funded an after-school monitor position the following year, at last relieving the staff of trying to police student behavior. Retired teacher Dick Murphy, well-versed in the ways of teenagers, created a model for this position, offering students help with homework, praising them when they were courteous, and firmly drawing the line when their "exuberance" reached unacceptable levels.

Late in 1997 Mary Soderberg retired after 22 years at Howe. She had been the first "new hire" in the new building and had progressed from part-time circulation assistant to supervisor of circulation services. At her retirement Mary was given a rocking chair and honored for her "calm, good cheer, and genuine helpfulness, no matter how hectic the pace." Her colleagues presented her with a hand-made quilt for which each had designed and made a square.

Kris Burnett completed work for her graduate degree in 1998 and was chosen as the new circulation supervisor. Jan Chapman joined the Howe staff, working part-time at the circulation desk. And Pam Soren,

Ruth Russell, beloved Library friend and volunteer, in whose memory a library scholarship was established

technical services assistant, began work on her graduate library degree with assistance from a continuing education scholarship fund for Howe staff endowed in Ruth Russell's memory. Ruth had been a beloved Library friend and volunteer, dispensing wit and tips on "good reads" as she checked out books to patrons.

In 1999 Ellen Lynch became assistant director when Peggy Hyde reduced her hours in preparation for retirement. Ellen brought her positive, thoughtful attitude and considerable library knowledge and organizational skills to her new leadership role.

That year the Town approved an additional 4.5 hours of staffing in technical services, bringing that department to a total of two full-time positions. This was a response to the unacceptable backlog of materials waiting to be processed for circulation, frustrating staff and creating impatience among patrons.

Several changes took place in the year 2000. Vicki Bedi resigned as head of technical services. Pam Soren Smith, having earned her master's degree, was promoted to that position; Joanne Blais returned to Howe as a public services librarian; and Peggy Hyde retired in April. She was honored at the reception opening the centennial history exhibit for her multiple contributions to the Library over 23 years and for "the warmth, humor, and generosity of spirit that are your hallmark."

Staff members still in place at the end of the decade also included Mary Hardy, Ann Schofield, Janice Grady, children's librarian Denise Reitsma, technical services assistant Mary Ryan, and circulation assistants Charlotte Bernini, Joan Ridgeway, Natalie Urmson, and Cindy Varnum.

Mary Hardy was now the senior reference librarian as well as head of collection management for adult materials. Ann Schofield's duties included selection of videos and classical music CDs along with reference and circulation work. Janice Grady's position as office manager included scheduling staff at the public service desks, bookkeeping, scheduling use of the meeting rooms, and Library correspondence.

Although there were many names on the staff roster in 2000, only seven of these were full-time employees. Library staffing at that point, in FTE's (full time equivalents) equaled 14.5, as compared with 6.75 FTE's in 1976 right after the move.

As the end of the Howe's first century drew near, the staff was poised to continue its tradition of providing a warm welcome and personal service to all ages, despite the overcrowding and the uncertainty about expansion/renovation or new construction. Marlene McGonigle stated,

> *"We envision a library that is flexible enough to function in a rapidly changing environment. That means planning for technology still unknown to us, while emphasizing that we are Hanover's living room, where the community is drawn to an environment that is comfortable and welcoming. The success of our ability to convey a sense of 'place' while at the same time incorporating access to information and materials, is the key to continued success of this public library."*

BANNER DESIGN: PRESENTATIONS, INC.

These banners celebrating the centennial hung on lamp posts along Main Street from September 1999 to April 2000.

THIRTEEN

Howe Library Turns One Hundred

1999 – 2000

As THE END of the century, and of the Library's first 100 years, drew near, certainly the most enjoyable item on the agenda for Board, Corporation and staff was planning for Howe's centennial celebration, which was to take place over several months. Under the leadership of Marilyn Crichlow, groups of volunteers worked on publicity, community events, special programs within the Library, and of course, the gala party that would mark the celebration's climax in April 2000.

Brainstorming began in late 1996. By early 1998 the centennial committee had done a survey to assess the public's perception of and knowledge about 1) Howe's services, 2) its status as an institution that relied on both public and private support, and 3) its need for expansion. They then began planning the celebration events and the strategies for publicizing both the events and Howe's need to grow in size to meet the new century's challenges.

A parallel committee, chaired first by Wayne Broehl and later by Cary Clark, worked on development planning, hoping to launch a capital fund for expansion on the 100th anniversary. This devel-

PHOTO BY PEGGY HYDE

COURTESY OF DARTMOUTH COLLEGE LIBRARY

"Emily Howe" (Priscilla Weismann) and "Hiram Hitchcock" (Leonard Morrissey, Jr.) leave the old library on West Wheelock Street to lead the centennial parade to the new library in a horse-drawn buggy, September 17, 1999.

PHOTO BY MARILYN CRICHLOW

Peggy Hyde and Priscilla Weismann (dressed as Emily Howe) stand near the exhibit "Our Century in Review." At left is Peggy's recreation of the wildflower table from Howe's early history.

opment committee worked with public relations consultants and launched a feasibility study. But when it became clear there could be no definite site decision by April 2000, they turned their energies to creating an annual fund that would build steady community financial support for Howe.

To spark public interest in the upcoming celebration, the centennial committee mailed newsletters to each household, spread publicity via the local media, and hung handsome banners with the message "Know Howe: 100 Years of Library Service" from Main Street lamp posts.

The kick-off parade on September 17, 1999 was a festive occasion that drizzling rain failed to subdue. Formally dressed in period costume, "Emily Howe" and "Hiram Hitchcock" (former Trustees

Priscilla Weismann and Leonard Morrissey) rode from the original building to the current site in a horse-drawn carriage, preceded by the Upper Valley Community Band and followed by balloon-toting celebrants of all ages. Upon arrival Emily and Hiram, with great ceremony, re-enacted the transfer of the deed that had begun Howe's story, after which the paraders sang "Happy Birthday" to the Library, enjoyed birthday cake, and reminisced about days of yore.

That fall, the Town having decided to feature Howe and its history in the Year 2000 calendar mailed to residents, Library staffer Kris Burnett worked to assemble old photos and a text for the calendar. The autumn series of centennial programs began; from October through March, Centennial Sundays at Howe featured seven varied programs presented by local speakers:

- *Hot Type was Hot Technology: The Gutenberg Bible and the Beginning of the Book*, by Professor Emeritus Charles Wood
- *Technology With Charm: The Electronic Book*, by Christian Sachs, vice-president of SoftBook Press
- *Random House, Scribners and Doubleday Are Not the Only Game in Town: Local Presses and Authors*, a panel moderated by Marisa Smith of Smith and Kraus Publishers
- *Besides Making Samplers: Women, Reading and Education*, by Professor Mary Kelley
- *Making Sense of Dollars: Using Library Resources to Find Investment Information*, a demonstration by the Howe reference staff
- *Treasures On Your Bookshelf*, a talk and old book appraisal by Stanley Brown, Curator of Rare Books at Dartmouth

- *Our Ten Favorite Books of the Century*, a discussion with local book club members.

Three special reading events were staged in February, March, and April:

- *The Greatest Novel of the 20th Century: James Joyce's Ulysses*, with selections read during the dinner hour at Murphy's Tavern by Professor James Heffernan
- *A Dr. Seuss Reading* at Thidwick's Kitchen, with a local school principal, a police officer, a minister, and a fire fighter among the readers
- *Hanover's Favorite Poems*, an evening of favorites read by representative Hanover residents.

Centennial programs for children included:

- a bookmark design contest, with the winners printed for distribution
- creation of a library mural at the Hanover Food Co-op by children in grades three to five
- designing of a "Libraries of Hanover" Valley Quest adventure by children in grades two to four
- three Saturday programs when children were invited to meet favorite authors Jesse Haas, Gloria Kamen, and Katherine Paterson and hear them read from their books
- a writing session for twelve to sixteen year olds, where young people were asked to illustrate or write poems or lyrics about pre-selected art works
- a family party with clown/mime/juggler Stephen Stearns, with guests invited to come dressed as a favorite storybook character.

Centennial Bookmark Design Contest:
winning bookmarks

Bryanne Leeming
Age 9

Haley Dodds
Age 9

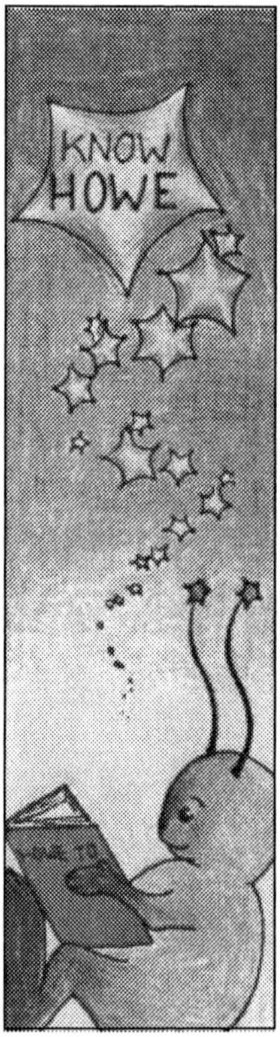

Sarah Douglas
Age 16

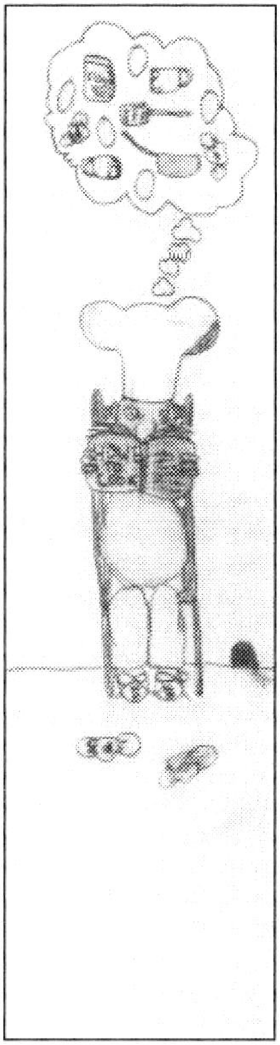

Cooper Dodds
Age 9

another bookmark page 195

Chris Whitney
Age 12

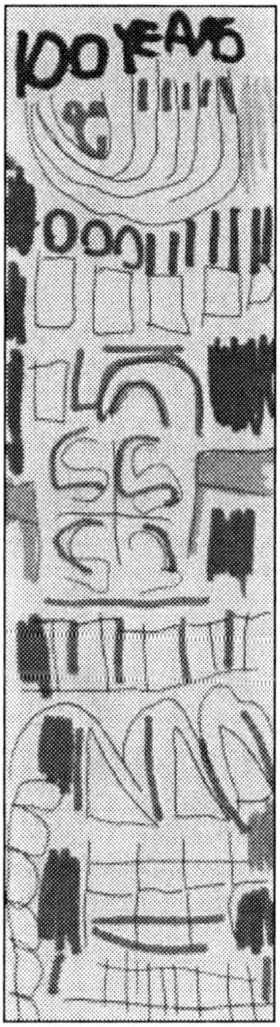

Nicholas Bernold
Age 5

On April 2, 2000, Howe held a public reception to open "Our Century in Review," a comprehensive historical exhibit covering Howe's first one hundred years. It was creatively designed by Peggy Hyde and Dick Ridgeway. This was Peggy's "last hurrah" at Howe, and she was honored with gifts and warm words of appreciation.

Finally, after this dazzling array of events, the centennial celebration's climax came on Sunday, April 9, 2000. The day's events began that afternoon in Dartmouth's Alumni Hall with a reading by Robert Pinsky, Poet Laureate of the United States. Mr. Pinsky had been the moving spirit behind the Favorite Poems Project of the Library of Congress—an audio and video archive of over 1,000 Americans reading and talking about their favorite poems, intended to "demonstrate through poetry where we stand at the beginning of a new millennium." He read from his own works and spoke with appreciation of what he had learned while encouraging Americans from all walks of life to share their deepest hopes and concerns through literature.

Dartmouth president James Wright, in his introduction of the program, reminded his audience of the Library's original setting in Eleazar Wheelock's former home. President Wright closed his remarks by saying, "Thus the histories of town and college have intertwined over the years. May they continue to thrive together in the next century."

That evening Robert Pinsky was guest of honor at a gala centennial dinner in the Daniel Webster Room of the Hanover Inn. He was introduced by Professor William Cook. Each of them paid tribute to the public library and to its role in their own lives and in American society. Their listeners, who shared warm memories of Howe's past and a loving concern for its future, were deeply moved by the remarks of these two men for whom libraries had been a life-long passion.

PHOTO BY ROBERT CRICHLOW

Poet Laureate Robert Pinsky chats with Professor William Cook at the centennial dinner.

It was an evening to be treasured—an elegant dinner graciously served, eloquent speakers whose words warmed their listeners' hearts, all of it shared with 150 of the Howe Library's oldest and truest friends. It seemed a perfect way for the Library to end its first 100 years as a vital Hanover presence and to carry Emily Howe's legacy into the next century.

Postscript

January 2003

By all measures, the Centennial Celebration served as a fitting culmination of Howe's first one hundred years. Now, two years later, several of the expansion conundrums left unanswered then have been resolved and planning moves forward.

First, a formal development program was put in place. An Annual Giving campaign was inaugurated in 2000, and ended successfully over the top at $82,943. The second campaign, in 2001, added another $82,054, and a like effort in 2002 was well along at this writing. In addition, a set of longer-term planned giving options have been put in place.

In 2002, with the Community Center under construction and decisions about schools nearly finalized, the site Dartmouth had considered offering Howe was found unworkable for reasons of expense and insufficient space for future growth. It then became obvious that the Library, involved for so long with other Town planning constituencies, was on its own.

Sentiment among Hanoverites was strongly in favor of Howe remaining downtown, preferably on its present site. The Trustees voted not to proceed further with the Robert Stern plan for expansion (which they felt was just not affordable), and began to interview other architectural firms. The architect chosen was Gerrit Zwart who, as a member of the Shepley Bulfinch Richardson and Abbott firm, had been the leader of the team designing Howe's present home.

As of this writing, concrete plans are moving forward for a significant expansion to provide some 30% more space. This will include a far bigger children's room, a special area for teens, and another for the burgeoning electronic efforts of the Library. (Already, the Library has adopted an update to the automated library system called "Millennium, " providing easy access to the Internet and extensive new electronic data bases.)

In addition to much-needed additional space for book stacks and seating, the new plan also includes more efficient staff working quarters and interesting new uses of Howe's outside space. Altogether, it promises a cornucopia of exciting new ideas.

To finance this imaginative yet practical expansion, the Howe Library Corporation is mounting a capital drive similar to that of the early 1970's, when the present building was constructed. It has pledged to raise, through this campaign, the funds required for the expanison/renovation. The Town of Hanover Selectmen and the Town Manager have continued their partnership with Howe, so well-developed in previous years.

Emily Howe had charged the Library to continue to serve the community "to the remotest generation," manifestly a wonderfully endless vision. Howe Library is now embarking on the second century of fulfilling that charge, and it continues to be a challenging and rewarding journey.

Wayne G. Broehl, Jr.
Howe Library Trustee, 1995–2002

Appendix A

Presidents of the Board of Trustees
1900 – January 2003

Hiram Hitchcock	1900
Charles P. Chase	1901 – 1924
Ashley K. Hardy	1925 – 1940
John B. Stearns	1941 – 1944
Fletcher Low	1945 – 1951
John B. Stearns	1952 – 1953
Robert J. Putnam	1954 – 1956
Louis O. Foster	1957 – 1961
Harry T. Schultz	1962 – 1963
Fletcher Low	1964
Harry T. Schultz	1965 – 1966
Christina Dickey	1967 – 1968
Elaine G. Harp	1969 – 1970
Barbara A. Morin	1971 – 1972
Mary S. Ermenc	1973 – 1974
Joan P. (Posey) Fowler	1975 – 1976
Ruth Young	1977 – 1978
Patricia H. Radway	1979 – 1980
Mary Ann H. Harris	1980 – 1981
Sharon L. Nordgren	1982
Peter F. Morrison	1983
Kathryn S. Manchester	1984 – 1985
Charles E. Widmayer	1986 – 1987
Charlotte Faulkner	1988 – 1990
John S. Stebbins	1991 – 1992
Margaret H. Otto	1993
W. David Goudy	1994 – 1995
Ann Crow	1995 – 1997
Matthew Marshall	1997 – 2001
Richard F. Winters	2001 –

Appendix B

Members of the Board of Trustees
1900 – January 2003

Perley R. Bugbee	1900 – 1935
Charles. P. Chase	1900 – 1924
Lucien B. Downing	1900 – 1914
Newton A. Frost	1900 – 1926
George H. Hitchcock	1900 – 1901
Hiram Hitchcock	1900
John K. Lord	1900 – 1916
Charles F. Richardson	1900 – 1911
William T. Smith	1900 – 1909
William Jewett Tucker	1900 – 1926
Henry J. Weston	1900 – 1903
Thomas W. D. Worthen	1900 – 1916
Frank Davison	1901 – 1911
Emily H. Hitchcock	1901 – 1912
Fanny H. Chase	1903 – 1934
Frank L. Janeway	1910 – 1911
Elizabeth C. Bugbee	1912 – 1924
Frederick P. Lord	1912 – 1946
Charles A. Proctor	1912 – 1929; 1931 – 1955
E. Lena Ward	1912 – 1915
Horace E. Hurlbutt	1915 – 1946
Harriet A. Storrs	1916 – 1918
Ashley K. Hardy	1917 – 1940
Harold G. Rugg	1917 – 1951
Mary A. Fletcher	1919 – 1949
William H. Murray	1924 – 1942
Edwin J. Bartlett	1925 – 1932
Eugene F. Clark	1927 – 1930
James P. Farnham	1927 – 1945
Robert J. Putnam	1930 – 1961
Theodore E. Bacon	1933 – 1953

Mrs. Gilman D. Frost	1933 – 1943
John B. Stearns	1936 – 1971
Fletcher Low	1941 – 1964
William Stuart Messer	1943 – 1952
Margaret B. McCallum	1944 – 1959; 1962 – 1970
Maurice C. Aldrich	1946 – 1977
Mrs. J. L. McDonald	1947 – 1957
Anton Raven	1948 – 1955
Leon B. Richardson	1950 – 1954
Robert D. Funkhouser	1952 – 1958
Margaret Sperry	1953 – 1972
S. John (Jack) Stebbins	1954 – 1977
Nathaniel Goodrich	1955 – 1958
Edwin Bailor	1956 – 1958
Louis O. Foster	1956 – 1962
Paul Stimson	1958 – 1965
Charlotte Morrison	1958 – 1960
Christina Dickey	1960 – 1963; 1965 – 1968
Harry T. Schultz	1960 – 1970
Herbert West	1960 – 1965
Christine Rand	1961 – 1969
Dorothy Leavitt	1962 – 1970
Catherine L. McKennan	1962 – 1971
Mary (Tay) Burnett	1963 – 1976
Donald Cameron*	1964 – 1966
Elaine G. Harp	1964 – 1977
Dorothy Sampson	1966 – 1968
Lewis J. Bressett	1967
Edward C. Lathem	1967 – 1987
David J. Bradley*	1968
William I. Crooker*	1969 – 1971
Joan P. (Posey) Fowler	1969 – 1991; 2002 –
Barbara A. Morin	1969 – 1977
Mary S. Ermenc	1970 – 1973
Dorothy J. Manchester	1971 – 1976
Patricia Robinson	1971

Colin D. Campbell	1972 – 1973
Donald W. Hawthorne*	1972 – 1977
Patricia H. Radway	1972 – 1983
John T. Schiffman	1972 – 1982
Mary Ellen Waters	1972 – 1975
Ruth Young	1972 – 1983; 1985 – 1994
Edgar T. Mead**	1974 – 1976
Jean Storrs**	1974
Alice B. Hayes**	1976 – 1981
Priscilla Weismann	1976 – 1979
Leonard E. Morrissey Jr.	1977 – 1994
Alice O. (Kate) Reed	1977 – 1983
Martha S. Solow*	1977 – 1980
Mary Ann H. Harris	1978 – 1985
John S. Stebbins	1978 – 1993
John F. Meck	1978
Peter F. Morrison	1979 – 1990
Sharon L. Nordgren	1979 – 1990
J. Peter Williamson	1979 – 1981
Jean G. Kruger	1980 – 1983
Marilyn (Willy) Black*	1982 – 1995
Kathryn S. Manchester	1982 – 1990
Elizabeth K. Smith**	1982 – 1984
Lawrence W. Draper	1983 – 1991
Kevin L. Carey	1984 – 1989
Charlotte Faulkner	1984 – 1990
Janet K. Hurd	1984 – 1989
Charles E. Widmayer	1984 – 1989
Frances Baschnagel	1988 – 1989; 1991 – 1996
Margaret A. Otto	1988 – 1996
Nardi R. Campion	1990
Ila Douple**	1990
Greydon Freeman	1990 – 1995
Richard Mayer	1990 – 1995
Douglas M. Bowen	1991 – 1993
J. Thomas Corindia	1991 – 1995

W. David Goudy	1991 – 1996
Clyde Watson	1991 – 1994
Ann Crow	1992 – 1997
Elizabeth Tobiasson	1992 – 1998
Ann S. Cioffi	1993 – 1998
Dale P. Bryant	1994 – 1999
Jay Heinrichs	1994 – 1995
Wayne G. Broehl, Jr.	1995 – 2002
Dorothy Heinrichs*	1995 – 1996
Stephen R. Marion	1995 – 2002
Matthew Marshall	1995 – 2001
Jean W. Whitall	1995 – 2001
Marjorie Boley	1996 – 2002
Jacqueline Clement	1996 – 2001
Phil Friedman	1996 – 1998
Brian F. Walsh*	1996 & 2000 –
Marilyn Crichlow	1997 –
John W. Manchester*	1997 – 1999
Betsy Storrs	1997 – 1999
Richard F. Winters	1997 –
Chris Vermilya	1998 – 1999
William B. Hamilton	1999 –
Edward Kerrigan	1999 –
Paul S. Olsen	1999 –
Jack Nelson	2000 –
Frederick Nothnagel	2000 –
William Geraghty	2001 –
Mado R. Macdonald	2001 –
Ralph Manuel	2001 –
Cheryl Boghosian	2002 –
Allegra B. Lubrano	2002 –
Leslie Williamson	2002 –

* On Board as Representative from Selectboard

** On Board as elected Trusteee of Town Library in Etna

Appendix C

Head Librarians
1900 – January 2003

Mabel Read	1900 – 1903
Lois Edith Chandler	1903 – 1905
Harriet A. Storrs	1905 – 1913
Etta M. Clark	1913 – 1923
Grace E. Kingsland	1923 – 1946
Elsie Lilly	1946 – 1949
Frances E. Haslett	1949 – 1951
Dorothy A. Hurlbutt	1952 – 1965
Joan G. Stewart	1965 – Sept. 1966
Mary Churchill (Acting)	Oct. – Dec. 1966
Patricia W. Eckels	Jan. 1967 – July 1987
Ann Trementozzi	Aug. 1987 – Nov. 1992
Peggy Forster Hyde (Acting)	Dec. 1992 – May 1994
Marlene F. McGonigle	May 1994 –

Appendix D

Members of the Library Staff
1900 – January 2003

Mabel Read	1900 – 1903
L. Edith Chandler	1903 – 1905
Harriet Storrs	1905 – 1913
Etta Clark	1913 – 1923
Dorothy Hurlbutt	1921 – 1937; 1951 – 1965
Grace Kingsland	1923 – 1946
Mrs. Perkins	? – 1940
Miss Little ‡	1931 – 1936
Miss Baker	1932 – 1942
Marian Jesseman ‡	1937 – 1942
Elizabeth Pillsbury	1940
Winifred Neef	1942
Mildred Fenton ‡	1943 – 1944
Elsie Lilly	1943 – 1949
Miss Clark	1946 – 1947
Adelaide Penberthy	1946 – 1947
Mary Steele Ermenc	1946 – 1947; 1952 – 1953
Joanne Pomeroy	1947 – 1949
Frances Haslett	1947 – 1952
Mary Churchill	1949 – 1992
Helen Garrison ‡	1949 – 1951
Iona Stimson	1949 – 1952
Mrs. Moench	1950 – 1951
Ruth Barlow ‡	1951 – 1952
Helen Stickney ‡	1952 – 1960
Frances Richmond	1952 – 1954
Mrs. William Bragner	1954 – 1958
Mabel Seavey	1957 – 1963

Joan Stewart	1958 – 1966
Elizabeth Hayward ‡	1960 – 1971
Mrs. Robert Kane	1963
Mrs. Albert Dekin	1965
Alene (Lari) Widmayer	1965 – 1971
Nancy Moorman	1966 – 1972
Patricia Eckels	1967 – 1987
Ann Byrne	1970 – 1972
Diane Haas	1971 – 1981
Pegge Strickler ‡	1971 – 1992
Elenita Chickering	1971 – 1975
Phyllis Phillips	1971 – 1975
Emily Duncan	1972 – 1976
Mary Ann Rupert	1974 – 1983
Mary Soderberg	1976 – 1997
Elizabeth Slive	1976 – 1977
Holly Porter	1977 – 1980
Eniko Gellai	1977 – 1982
Polly Gould	1981 –
Lurlene Cole	1982 – 1989
Peggy Hyde	1980 – 2000
Charlotte Bernini	1984 –
Marcia Manzo	1983 – 1987
Jean Watson	1983 – 1994
Ellen Lynch	1983 – 1986; 1992 –
Ann Schofield	1984 –
Mary Hardy	1986
Cindy Varnum	1982 –
Kit Farrell	1984 – 1996
Pamela Marshall	1985 – 1987
Natalie Urmson	1986 –
Joan Ridgeway	1987 – 1989; 1993 –
Ann Trementozzi	1987 – 1992

Hillary Platt	1988 – 1993
Janice Blake Grady	1988 –
Joanne Blais ‡	1992 – 1998; 2000 –
Rob Sargent	1992 – 1994
Victoria Bedi	1993 – 1999
Marlene McGonigle	1994 –
Pamela Soren Smith	1994 –
Mary Ryan	1995 –
Amelia Talbert	1995 –
Kristina Burnett	1996 –
Jan Chapman	1998 –
Denise Reitsma ‡	1998 –
Christine Eickelman	2000 –
Meredith Bird Miller	2000 – 2001
Mary Catherine Jones	2002
Susan Milord	2002 –

‡ Children's librarian

Because there are no conclusive records of staff names until 1966, the listing for earlier years is incomplete.

Appendix E

Named Endowment Funds

Name of Fund	*Year Established*
Hattie Abbott	1977
Maurice Aldrich	1978
Dorothy Gile Brackett	1988
Michael K. Broehl	1984
Dagmar Clark	1997
Norma W. Fisk	1992
Dorothy Forster	1991
Joan P. Fowler	1985
Anne Slade Frey	1993
Adelaide Hardy	1965
Evelyn Hansen Hurd	1987
Vaughn Lawrence Jenkyn	1997
Grace Kingsland	1973
Jean G. Krueger	1984
Edward Connery and Elizabeth French Lathem	1981
Elizabeth French Lathem	1992
Sony Lipton	1993
Joseph L. McDonald	1981
Catherine Laycock McKennan	1985
Meck-Hazlett	1963
Malcolm Mellor	1991
Elizabeth Skolfield Miller	1995
Gertrude Rogers Moody	1985
Mildred Morse	1986
Elden Murray	1977
Hazel M. Nelson	1991

MABEL READ	1906
RUTH RUSSELL	1992
W. K. AND ETHEL STEWART	1965
JOHN H. STRICKLER	1983
KATE AND GUSTAVUS TUCKERMAN	1996
JAMES WICKER LIBRARIAN'S DISCRETIONARY FUND	1975
CHARLES E. WIDMAYER	1991
REBECCA G. WILLIAMS	1991
JEAN M. WITHERELL	1983
JOHN H. AND JOSEPHINE WOLFENDEN	1990
GERTRUDE B. WRIGHT	1980

Molly Mamourian
Age 10